The Second Flowering of Emily Mountjoy

The Second Flowering of Emily Mountjoy

Joan Lingard

ST. MARTIN'S PRESS
NEW YORK

The publisher acknowledges the financial assistance of
The Scottish Arts Council in the publication of this volume

The publishers are grateful to the Executors of the
Eugene O'Neill estate for permission to reproduce
the extracts from *Long Day's Journey into Night*

Library of Congress Cataloging in Publication Data

Lingard, Joan.
  The second flowering of Emily Mountjoy.

  I. Title.
PZ4.L755Se 1980   [PR6062.I493]   823'.9'14   79-22791
ISBN 0-312-70833-5

FOR MARTIN
with much love

Chapter One

FARQUHAR Mountjoy, Writer to the Signet, stood by the long window in his office. Behind him the room soared upwards in Georgian proportions to terminate in beautifully worked cornices and a central ceiling rose. Once people had dined here under chandeliers; now he worked at the long desk stacked with deeds under a light bulb in a plastic shade.

It was twelve minutes to noon. He knew the time exactly. He had checked it only two minutes before and in two minutes' time he would pull the old silver watch from his pocket and check it again. He was neither nervous nor agitated. He had waited for too many noons to strike.

He watched a woman with a dog open the gate of the private garden in the middle of the crescent and go inside. Not much of a day for walking in gardens. The paths looked like ribbons of mud, the grass would be a swamp. Through the black iron railings and thin bare trees the woman remained visible, her red coat making a bright stab of colour in the midst of such colourlessness. In high summer the gardens were bursting with greenery, and then they were private. He had played in them as a boy; his aunt had lived on the opposite side of the crescent, and now his two elder sisters did, in the same house. He himself had moved out to the suburbs when he married in order to be detached and to enjoy the amenities of a large walled garden and double garage. There was no doubt but that a good garden and a garage raised the value of a property.

Property was in his blood, and had been ever since he concluded his first sale as a very young solicitor. The flat had had nothing spectacular about it but he had enjoyed every step of the transaction from first receiving the clients and their instructions to the moment at twelve midday when the offers arrived

7

and he had opened them solemnly, slitting each one with the silver paper knife which still lay on his desk, to find that they had done exceedingly well, much better than his clients had hoped. From then on he had looked at the city of Edinburgh, its streets and houses, with a new eye. And so he had come to specialise in property, which occupied his time apart from a few other minor undertakings such as the preparing of wills and their execution. He left the court work to his partner, much of which these days was divorce work, an aspect of legal practice he himself had little stomach for. He hated the sordid details of other people's private lives. He hated the distress. Houses were less messy.

He pulled out the watch which had been his grandfather's. Leaving ten to. The woman in red was coming out of the garden now, jerking the unwilling dog behind her. It raised its leg against the gatepost. She shivered, put up the collar of her coat.

Another woman was coming along the pavement hunched into a dark cloak-like garment. A small child clung to her hand which was invisible beneath it. They were coming up the steps to the office. He saw the droop of her mouth and absent stare of her eyes and knew they would be going to see his partner.

In the adjoining room the telephone rang twice before his secretary silenced it. His buzzer went. He moved swiftly to his desk and lifted the receiver.

'Farquhar Mountjoy here.'

'I was wondering, Farquhar – '

'Emily!'

At once she retreated, saying she was sorry, shouldn't she have phoned just now, was it a bad moment? He took a deep breath before he answered her.

'Do you realise it is seven minutes to *twelve*, Emily?'

Obviously she had not, and she had not realised either that it was a closing day, although he had mentioned it at breakfast. She said that she had better not keep him then in case he lost the sale of the century. She put down the receiver. He stared at the black mouthpiece in his own hand. Drops of moisture encircling the rim made him wrinkle his nose with distaste. He banged it back on its cradle. Emily was behaving most oddly these days; it was if she was away in a dream. Gone with the fairies,

8

his old nurse who used to wheel him through the gardens might have said.

Now it was five minutes to. Only two white unopened envelopes lay on his desk. He had expected three, and the one which was missing was the one which his instinct told him would be highest. But there was still time. Some lawyers liked to put in their bids at the very last second; he himself preferred to leave a margin for delay and sent a runner normally at half past eleven, as he had done this morning, to McWhirter, McKay and McIndoe. Some lawyers too, he was well aware, might open the envelopes before twelve, and a small few might even try then to do a little spot of bumping up the price. A quick phone call and an eager purchaser might like to change a figure. Not he. His dealings were strictly honourable. He was known for it, would never divulge a detail about a client's personal or business life. One must be able to look oneself in the mirror, he had decided early on; in fact, there had been no conflict, no struggle against the temptations of the devil, for the devil had never tempted him.

A sharp knock on the door brought him to it at once. A runner handed in the third white envelope. Farquhar Mountjoy went to the connecting door and said, 'Miss Lyall, it is almost twelve.'

He put the third letter beside the others in order of arrival. Miss Lyall, who had been with him for twenty-seven years, entered, her spectacles hanging from her neck on a gold chain. She was smiling. He was always conscious of her smile for smiling was not common in this crescent.

The hands of the silver pocket watch were almost together at the top. He watched the second hand ticking its way relentlessly round the face. He knew it was not strictly necessary to be quite so punctilious, he even made a little fun of himself for being so, but it had become a part of the ritual. Outside in the misty air, the clocks began to strike across the city. The second hand was pointing north.

'I think we may allow ourselves to look now, Miss Lyall.'

He lifted the first envelope, slit it neatly across. One thousand and fifteen pounds over the upset price. He laid it aside. Miss Lyall was holding the next envelope out for him. The second offer was two thousand five hundred and fifty-three over.

9

And the third, five thousand two hundred and twenty-two above the upset! He had known that offerer had been keen, having already offered for five houses unsuccessfully.

'Splendid!'

'Congratulations, Mr Mountjoy.'

Immediately he lifted the telephone and rang the winning solicitor. And that was it. The deal was sealed, and would be confirmed immediately in writing. A man's word was his bond, which was how it should be. He found English clients were often disconcerted by the Scottish method of buying and selling property; they did not like the blind bidding, having to guess what the other person might be doing. But in England people could offer and back away; their word could not be trusted. Gazumping was rife.

'We do things differently in Scotland,' he would tell them. 'And, I believe, better.'

A moment later the telephone rang again. McWhirter, McKay and McIndoe, to tell him that his client had been successful, and his bid had only been ninety-nine pounds over the upset. The client had wished to bid more to make sure, had rung at ten in a flurry of anxiety to say increase the offer, but he had cautioned him to stay calm and not get carried away, and to trust his judgment.

'A good morning, Mr Mountjoy,' said Miss Lyall.

'Indeed,' said Farquhar Mountjoy.

After lunch, Farquhar Mountjoy's wife drove into town with her friend Mrs Seton. Their journey was of the lurching variety, made up of hectic rushes and sudden stops. Mrs Seton drove with vulgar verve, the only activity in her life which contained any element of vulgarity. In a car she became a changed woman. Emily Mountjoy was glad when they came to rest at the north end of the Grassmarket.

'Poor Mrs McCreedy,' sighed Mrs Seton, as they got out of the car. 'Look, there goes her son!' She stabbed the air with a broad, sheepskinned finger. Sheep wool also encircled her wrists and thick throat. 'Conal McCreedy, the actor.'

Emily Mountjoy, wrapped in beaver against the damp January

afternoon, eased her neck sideways so that she might watch the young man advancing up the pavement on their right-hand side.

'He looks very Irish.'

'Oh, it's difficult to say what Conal is. He was born and bred up there!' This time the finger went upwards, pointing to the top of the tenement which was their destination. Then, swivelling their eyes to the right, they saw the castle sitting sternly upon its high rock, keeping guard.

Now they looked back down at Conal McCreedy who was passing an antique shop and a group of slumped down-and-outs, paying no attention to anyone or anything; he walked with head down, a stack of books under his arm. He reached the corner of the West Bow, rounded it to go up Victoria Street and was lost from their sight. Emily Mountjoy had a crick in her neck. She revolved it gently inside its fur collar. She was sure she must have a touch of arthritis. Only to be expected really. Nothing lasted for ever.

'Well, shall we go?'

They crossed to the pavement, Mrs Seton leading the way. She was taking her friend to be introduced to Mrs McCreedy. She herself had been a customer for many years and had guarded her 'treasure' closely in the way that one did out-of-the-way holiday paradises, eulogising but not revealing. As soon as one revealed, the value dropped. Sandy beaches were quick to fill. But Mrs McCreedy had asked if she would have a friend she might recommend, for one customer had died, another moved away, and yet another, with a shift in fortune, was suddenly having to buy her clothes in Princes Street chain stores. Mrs Mountjoy, when approached, had been most grateful.

On the pavement, obstructing their path, sat a woman, a meths drinker from the look of her glazed eyes, slack, rag-doll limbs, and the stream of wetness issuing from between her legs. They averted their eyes, out of embarrassment and compassion, only to find themselves confronted by another of her kind, a man, who stared at them with such blank madness that they did a quick sidestep and circled round him to arrive at Mrs McCreedy's stair door. It was said that such people were harmless, too far gone, but one could never be quite sure. There was little one could be sure of nowadays. Once upon a time you could even leave your back door unlocked in the daytime.

'Skid row, eh?' smiled Mrs Seton. She grew more serious. 'Terrible though that they should be allowed to hang about in the city centre.'

Emily Mountjoy realised that it was years since she had read Steinbeck, been engaged by, and even identified with, his characters. Had she really done that? She paused to look back at the man and woman. She realised too it was years since she had set foot in the Grassmarket. How strange, considering it was right in the heart of the city. Once she had combed its junk and antique shops, but she had enough antiques now, had lost interest somehow, was no longer excited by 'finds'; and junk she no longer needed. Her daughter's life revolved around junk.

Her friend was looking round, anxious to get a move on.

They entered the stair. The walls were filthy, as if they had been smeared with coal dust, amongst other substances. They walked firmly up the middle of the passage.

'Mrs McCreedy is quite a character, you know.'

'So you have always said.'

They began the long climb upward. It was many years since Emily Mountjoy had been in such a stair either. It fairly took her back: the steep, grey worn steps dipping in the middle misleading the eye, the smell of damp, cat and urine, and the gloom. The gloom was the worst aspect: it penetrated the spirit so immediately. She wondered if she would like to come alone, was surprised that her friend had done so all these years, braving the dim light and dark corners, passing scuffed doors which might open up to disclose all manner of disturbing possibilities. She shivered, shrinking deeper in to her beaver.

Every now and then they came upon some light heralding a verandah running off on the right-hand side, on which strings of washing dangled lifelessly. It was one of those unusual Edinburgh days without wind. They saw an inert ginger cat but no person, and heard no sound but that of their heartbeats. They had to rest twice, for Mrs McCreedy lived high up, and they were not as young as they used to be.

At length, outside Mrs McCreedy's door, they halted, to gather breath, re-settle their fur and sheep wool, pat up the backs of their hair. As soon as they were composed, Mrs Seton took a long pull on the brass bell. They listened to its tinkle dying away inside the flat. It brought back more echoes to Emily Mountjoy.

The door was opened two inches at first, then the aperture widened and Mrs McCreedy was revealed. Emily Mountjoy extended a plump, ringed hand.

'At last!' she cried gaily. She felt as if she had drunk a glass of sherry too fast or ascended too sharply in a lift.

The little dressmaker said nothing, the thick pebble glass of her spectacles glinted up at them, then the squat body encased in its navy blue and white polka dots went ahead of them through the narrow lobby into her room. The spots danced before Emily Mountjoy's eyes. She rubbed them so that she could see the room more clearly. It was an exotic, silken haven perched on high; thus she described it on the following day to her husband who, considering his wife prone to exaggeration, merely nodded absentmindedly. Every chair, ledge, table, was draped with bales of silk and satin, lace and soft, pure wool, of colours that ranged from the palest milky pinks and blues to the deepest flaming reds and oranges. Mrs McCreedy would not sew with man-made fibres and her customers knew better than to offer sludgy colours or lurid abstract designs.

In the fireplace, black-bricked and brass-fendered, glowed a coal fire. Mrs McCreedy was obviously a woman of few compromises. How lovely to see a real fire! cried Emily Mountjoy, wondering if she had remembered to take her blood-pressure pill after lunch. She most certainly felt strange. Could it be the altitude? She edged towards the window. The street did seem a long way down to her who lived in a two-storeyed house. Or was it that she was seeing everything in a slightly distorted fashion this afternoon? She looked up towards the market cross and the memorial for the Covenanters and the public lavatory and the group of down-and-outs. They were everywhere. Oh, not where she lived of course! Not yet at least. But they had had to shut the men's lavatory in the public library because of them, she had heard. She put her hand to her head. Who could have told her that? She looked back at the fire, at its warm enticing glow, moving instinctively closer. Central heating was all very well, marvellous for keeping the back warm, but it didn't do too much for the full frontal. Full frontal? What *was* going on in her head this afternoon?

'You have a splendid view, Mrs McCreedy,' she said, for she must always say something, said her husband, and although she recognised that to be true could not resist the impulse. Compulsive commenting. She supposed it was a sign of some neurotic trend but did not wish to have her suspicions confirmed. And now that she had made her comment she could not help wondering if it had been a foolish and even tactless one for the little dressmaker's glasses were so thick that it was a miracle she could still see to sew, let alone to expect her to be able to see the view. For years, at Merchant Company dinners, golf-club dinner dances, and pre-Sunday lunch cocktail parties, Mrs Seton had been declaring that it was truly a miracle, until Mrs McCreedy had begun to seem like a runner-up to the Virgin Mother herself. Her eyes must now be in her fingers. Amazing how people compensated. They all knew *that*, one way or another.

And thinking of miracles, Emily Mountjoy's eyes went back to the only disturbing object in the room, that of a large (surely unnecessarily large?) wooden replica of Christ hanging from the cross above the fireplace. His suffering looked enormous. Her Presbyterian soul blenched, in spite of her long attachment to the idea of church unity.

A bale of ice white satin was lifted from a pale green chaise longue, and the two women seated themselves. Mrs Seton began to engage the dressmaker in conversation, about her son. The change in his mother was perceptible: her mouth relaxed into a smile, her eyes stirred to life behind their heavy screens, the whole of her small, square body slackened, as if lapped by heat.

'He's an actor, I believe?' put in Emily Mountjoy.

Mrs McCreedy waved her hand at the walls and let the photographs tell their own tale. Mrs Mountjoy got up to examine them. There he was as Hamlet, Peer Gynt, Joe Keller in *All My Songs*, Macbeth, Tregorin in *The Seagull*, Ernest in *The Importance of Being Earnest*. Smiling, frowning, laughing, gay, exultant, abject, he covered the walls. The dark eyes were engaging and demanding, the mouth full and sensual. Yes, it was most definitely sensual, decided Mrs Mountjoy, leaning forward from the waist to make a closer examination; and sensitive.

'He is obviously very versatile,' she murmured.

'He could play anything,' said his mother.

'Is he busy at the moment?' asked Mrs Seton.

He was appearing at the Church Hill Theatre that evening, said his mother, in *Long Day's Journey Into Night*, and tomorrow he was filming in the Borders with the B.B.C. They were doing *Kenilworth* for yet another of their serials. They were so good on the Classics, said Mrs Seton approvingly, for she preferred the old over the new, in almost everything. How thrilling, exclaimed Emily Mountjoy, meaning Conal's involvement with the B.B.C. rather than the B.B.C.'s with the Classics, and already she could feel, despite her avowed aversion for the romantic, a stirring of passion at the thought of horsebeats thudding through the misty Border air and the spirit of Sir Walter hanging over all. She had always meant to go back and read him, from the advantage of maturity, and once had tried with *Ivanhoe* but, unable to recapture the old thrill, had laid it aside with a National Trust bookmark between two yellowed pages, and there it had rested ever since.

'And who is Conal to be?' She allowed her tongue to linger over his name.

Oh, he had just a small part, said his mother dismissively. There was a terrible lot of favouritism in that world, you know, and it was a case of whom you knew rather than who you were. Trite but true. Oh yes! Dear, but the things she could tell them? Corruption, sighed Mrs Seton. Wasn't it awful the way it invaded every aspect of life nowadays? She had to check her butcher's bills when ten years ago the thought wouldn't have entered her mind. Emily Mountjoy gazed at the dark, laughing eyes of Conal McCreedy and wondered whom her husband might know in that line. He was a member of the Arts Club, amongst others. She must have a word with him.

'You know all about that world though, don't you, Mrs McCreedy? I mean from personal experience.'

Thus encouraged, the dressmaker embarked on a few of her

theatrical anecdotes – most of her ladies liked those thrown in with the fitting – telling of her life before marriage behind the curtains at the Opera House in Belfast and then at the Gaiety in Dublin and the King's Theatre in Edinburgh. She had been a wardrobe mistress, had enjoyed the pantomimes best, was not like Conal who had more highbrow tastes, but then he had had the benefits of a good education. Her listeners nodded approvingly. Mrs McCreedy had paid for him to be educated at a well-known boys' school in the city. 'It gave him a bit of class, I will say that.' Stick in at your lessons, she used to tell him, not needing to add that she was sewing her fingers to the bone to pay for them, but he had not stuck in entirely successfully, not in terms of academic qualifications, although he was intelligent, there was no denying that.

'The theatre must have been in his blood,' said Mrs Mountjoy. 'His father was an actor too, so I understand from Mrs Seton?'

'Actor? Him!' Mrs McCreedy laughed. She had met him one summer when she went to Dun Laoghaire for her holidays. That was the end of Mary Macgillicuddy! Gerry McCreedy had been nothing but a small-time entertainer working in a summer show. The warm-up man. 'Good name for him. All he *could* do was warm up. As soon as the heat got too much he'd take off as if he'd skates on his feet. Oh, he'd a great pair of heels on him, there's no denying that. Last time I saw the back of them was when I told him Conal was on the way. That was when he was in a panto at the King's. Left everybody in the lurch. Day before Christmas Eve it was. He could talk though, I will say that for him. Well, you might have guessed as much. He must have had something, mustn't he? But he never listened. Trying to tell him anything was like trying to sup porridge with a knitting needle.'

Emily Mountjoy could have sat on the chaise longue before the fire and listened to Mrs McCreedy telling her things all day long. She felt mesmerised. It was a while since she had felt the pitch of her nerves to have dropped so low.

'Why did *you* give up the theatre, Mrs McCreedy?' she asked.

Briskly, Mrs McCreedy said that she had not wanted to bring Conal up in a sewing hamper or any of that nonsense, with chorus girls popping bits of chocolate into his mouth every time they passed. Nor did she want him to follow in his father's footsteps. No mother would have wished that on any son of Gerry McCreedy.

Then she brought them to the point of their coming, for she could not whittle afternoons away, as they might. Reluctantly, Mrs Mountjoy swam upward from her trance-like state, and produced her material, a summer print for a sun dress. She and her husband were planning to go to Corfu in May and she must be made to look presentable for the beach, if that were possible. Her laugh was tinkly and self-mocking. She stood up to remove her outer garments, glancing nervously towards the window even though she knew they were not overlooked. She stood before the fire in her slip, with one hand protectively covering her cleavage. The skin between her breasts had begun to pucker and sag. Her breasts would sag too if she did not holster them up so tightly. At night-time, when she released them, she had to massage the deep red marks left by their bonds. She felt vulnerable standing there revealing so much flesh to other women after so many years of showing herself – and even then she knew how to whisk clothes on and off with minimum exposure – only to Farquhar. Anyway, he never seemed to be looking, not nowadays; not for a long time.

The dressmaker took the inchtape from her neck and spanned it around Mrs Mountjoy's breasts.

'Rather large, I'm afraid.' The customer was apologetic.

But most of Mrs McCreedy's customers were generously endowed, as she always termed it, for them, and, indeed, that was one of the reasons they came to her, so she did not express any shock when the tape met at forty-six inches. She had no intention of going metric. She took a short pencil from behind her ear and noted the measurement down in her notebook, opening up a new page for Mrs Mountjoy. Momentarily abandoned, the latter glanced sideways and saw herself reflected in a full-length mirror. The revelation produced in her a sudden tremor of shock. Quickly, she looked away.

They heard the flat door opening.

'That'll be Conal,' said his mother, on her knees, spanning now the wide hips.

A new tremor afflicted Mrs Mountjoy, causing her breasts and upper arms to tremble, and then she felt the old hot flush rising up from the depths of her cleavage to fire her neck.

'It's all right – he won't come in.'

And all the while Mrs Seton sat back against the end of the chaise longue, one arm resting on the rail, watching.

The measurements were recorded, and Mrs Mountjoy thankfully pulled on her dress, allowing her friend to zip her up the back. She combed her hair in front of the long mirror, re-powdered her cheeks with a greenish powder from a tortoiseshell compact, resolved to go back on the low carbohydrate diet, and read *Kenilworth*. Mrs Seton was saying that she was sure Mrs Mountjoy would like to meet Conal. 'Wouldn't you, Emily?' Emily murmured, and his mother went to fetch him.

Emily Mountjoy turned back to the room. She felt bewitched by it, by its warmth and texture. It made her feel languid and created in her the desire to touch everything. She ran her hand over the soft pile of an apricot-coloured velvet chair and experienced a shiver on her spine as if someone had whispered close to it.

When Conal entered she felt a startling desire to touch him also. It was seldom that one saw such a beautiful man. He was dark-haired and dark-eyed, and he moved with an easy grace and smiled with an easy manner. He was not as young as he had appeared in the street, but he was not old either. Certainly not as old as she. She moved forward, blushed, remembering herself, and stepped back.

He was extending his hand, declaring it to be a pleasure to meet Mrs Seton again and he was delighted, too, to meet his mother's new client. Mrs Mountjoy noticed that her friend's face, normally quite colourless, had taken on a slight tinge of pink, and she was talking and laughing with unusual animation.

Mrs McCreedy had a finger on her opened diary, and was eyeing the clock on the mantelpiece.

'We must go!' cried Mrs Seton. 'We've taken up enough of your time, Mrs McCreedy. It's always the same, isn't it? Your room is so very seductive.'

Another appointment was made for Mrs Mountjoy, further

handshakes were exchanged, the room swirled with activity, and then the two women left, with backward glances, leaving the smells of their bodies and perfumes behind them. After an afternoon of fittings Mrs McCreedy had to push up the window and let in the wind to clean out the air. For a few minutes she would allow it to ruffle the edges of her silks and satins and she would listen to the roar of the rush-hour traffic below before bringing the window back down and securing it for the night. In the evening hours she liked to feel the room belonged exclusively to her. Conal was seldom home before midnight; that was when they had their time together, eating, partaking of a dram or two of malt whisky, smoking, talking. He talked mostly, about his plays and the people he met, and she listened, nodding, watching him. They were night people, both, and they loved the stillness of the night around them and the feeling that the city was sleeping, whilst they snuggled deep inside their warm, glowing eyrie. They heaped the fire high so that it sparked and spat with life. They let it burn far into the night. They enjoyed storms too, as well as stillness, when rain battered and drove against their windows, and the wind prowled around their high tenement.

Thinking of Conal and his mother, and their little flat in the Grassmarket, Emily Mountjoy went home to her house on the Braid Hills, from which she enjoyed a marvellous view of the city on clear days. Today was grey and misty. She hung up her fur coat, took off her shoes, and in stockinged feet padded through her solid, plush house. It was detached, late Victorian, of no particular architectural merit, and certainly no historical interest, but it was roomy and comfortable to bring up a family in. Six beds, three reception, and all the other usual offices. All was in order, as it had been when she went out after lunch. The floors were polished, the curtains lined, the reproduction furniture unchipped, and the antique suitably displayed. No tap dripped, no grease clung behind the cooker, no nasty smells wrinkled the nose, and no noise assailed the ears except for the hum made by the fridge and the central-heating boiler. Her feet made no sound on the velvet-piled Wilton. Even the road outside was hushed, for it was not time yet for the men to return from town. Her daily help had gone at midday. And her son James had gone last year, to Vancouver.

Her daughter Camilla had gone three months ago, to Stockbridge, on the other side of the city. She was living in a flat which smelt of incense and patchouli oil with a young man who was fairly dirty even by those standards. They sat on the floor, rolled cigarettes, drank beer from the can and ate 'real' food. Emily Mountjoy had done her best to like him and not to disapprove of the arrangement. She visited them, taking wholemeal bread and French cheese, for Mr Mountjoy would not have them in his house. Her daughter, without meaning especially to insult and not in any outburst of temper, had told her mother she was so bourgeois she was afraid to change a hair of her head or a line of her body. She would do anything rather than disturb the status quo or threaten her meal ticket. Mr Mountjoy said that Camilla talked a lot of stuff and nonsense, all her ideas were borrowed and not even understood, since she didn't have a brain in her head and they had always known it. He had hoped the spending of so much money on her education might have done something for her, might at least have given her a taste for culture or put a bit of polish on her. Of course they knew their situation *vis-à-vis* their children was by no means unique and it became boring to go on about it.

But Conal McCreedy had stayed with his mother. He both loved *and* respected her: you could see it in the way he looked at her, hear it in the way he talked to her, not using the harsh aggressive tone she heard so often in Camilla's voice. She seemed to exasperate and irritate her daughter, and yet she had loved her so much, cherished, encouraged, tried not to spoil, to bring her up thoughtfully. They said that if you loved them everything would turn out all right in the end. But love had turned out to be not enough.

Yes, she was afraid, she admitted to herself, as she slumped heavily into a linen-covered tub chair. She stared at the damask drapes. Her daughter had hessian at her windows and a bed bought from the 'lane' sales that smelt of dried urine. She had gone with Camilla on a couple of occasions to the alleyway that ran along the back of George Street and examined with distaste which she could not suppress, the sodden pillows, ratty carpets, chipped china, worm-eaten, disintegrating wardrobes. The people there had looked just as sodden and worm-eaten, like characters left over from Dickens, haggard, ferret-faced, scabbed and rouged, poking, picking, scratching. The seediness she had found not at all colourful and this had given Camilla yet another opportunity to harangue her on her favourite tack.

The vision of the dressmaker's room came back, superimposing itself on her own understated, quiet-toned drawing room, so that it seemed to have more reality. She felt the heat of the fire, the touch of the velvet, saw Conal's dark eyes. She might have been like Mrs McCreedy, living a life like hers, with some variation of course since she could not see herself dressmaking, but basically the same, she with a child, rearing him alone, independent of a man and a social position to keep up. She might have had a room of her own, gleaming and shining, filled with things of her own choosing. There would have been just the two of them which might have been better in the end – well, better for her at least – since they would have been close and he might not have been so quick to get away. A lot of trivia would have been stripped from her life. At once the rational part of her added : and a lot of other kinds might have taken its place. Was it possible to live without it? Almost certainly not. But what if one's life consisted only of trivia? The thought arrested her and she could not bear the pain of thinking any further.

The telephone rang, providing distraction. Eagerly, she seized the receiver, but the caller was only Farquhar to say that he would be late home, something about an important client from out of town trying to buy a grouse moor. She did not need to listen for he always spoke in the same phrases, used the same words. She found it difficult to believe that much of his business must be carried on after five o'clock but had never queried it. She could not be bothered. Perhaps he had a fancy woman. She doubted it though, being unable to imagine it. She could not visualise him sitting in a dark corner of a restaurant looking into the eyes of his toothsome secretary. Poor Miss Lyall, who had devoted her life to him and her mother who was ninety years and and still showed no sign of giving up ! Besides, he wore the most dilapidated underwear and resisted all his wife's efforts to provide new – he was prudent when it was an item which was not visible – and she thought that if he was having an affair with another woman he would be unlikely to present himself in such old-fashioned, dis-coloured shorts. A friend had told her that it was when her husband began purchasing numerous pairs of fancy underpants she began to suspect him of infidelity. Fancy woman. The expression came from her daily help whose neighbours all seemed to have or, to be, fancy women. Fancy is as fancy does. Whatever tickles your fancy. Did anything tickle hers?

'Emily? Are you there?'

'Yes, I am here, Farquhar.' And where else would she be?

'Are you all right? You sound a bit – well, never mind. I'll try not to be too late home but don't keep dinner.'

It didn't matter, she told him, he could be as late as he wished for she was perfectly all right. Replacing the receiver, she said aloud, 'Of course I'm all right.' The words spoken into the still room disturbed her, in the way that looking in Mrs McCreedy's mirror had. She looked over her shoulder. She was alone.

The hot flush was rising up her neck again and she felt as if she was about to suffocate. She gasped for breath. Stumbling to the window she unlocked the burglar snib and flung up the heavy glass with all her strength, then leant out into the garden and took deep breaths of air which was heavy with the smell of wet earth. Her fingers gripped the sill. She must stop feeling sorry for herself. People were dying in Ulster and the Middle East, starving in India. None of that helped, of course. It was just so much infor-mation, even though one was moved by pictures of weeping rela-tives and pot-bellied children with large imploring eyes. She remembered seeing the first pictures that came out of Belsen and being shocked and sick right to the middle of her being but so much had happened since then and the horrors had been so terrible that one could not afford to feel that degree of shock any longer. Over the years the senses had blunted. But what could one do? She worked in a charity shop two mornings a week. Sometimes, sorting second-hand clothes, she thought about the starving children. She was starving, in her own way; dying too. She felt the seeds of decay in her, the disintegration of body and spirit. It was the break-up of the spirit that was the worst thing.

She felt that hers was in limbo wandering around in some great void, disassociating itself from her. Even her belief in God had gone this past while although she still went to church on Sundays and stood in the pew beside Farquhar holding her navy-blue hymnbook between her gloved hands. Last Sunday she had had to resist the temptation to scream in the middle of the Hundredth psalm. *His mercy is for ever sure . . .*

The woman across the road was watching from her upstairs window. Glancing up, she caught her eye, and the woman busied herself with rearranging the curtain.

Pull yourself together, Emily Mountjoy! This would never do. She took a last breath of air and pulled in her head. Now she must *do* something. Go out. Eat, drink and be merry! Self-pity was the most disgusting of all the sins.

She went upstairs and put her fur coat and shoes back on.

She locked the front door three times with different keys (they were in a prime house-breaking area), went into the garage and sat in her car. She put the key into the ignition, watched it dangle. Where could she go? To visit Camilla? She shrank from the idea; she needed to feel strong when she went there. She might go and have a meal somewhere but she had never eaten out in a restaurant on her own except for the occasional quick lunchtime snack.

She would have to go somewhere.

Slowly, she drove down the hill to Morningside, taking time, hoping for sudden inspiration, expecting none. They did not have the kind of friends one dropped in on, not that there was anyone she wanted to see right now. She thought of Mrs McCreedy but could not go back and disturb her in her warm silken nest. Lucky Mrs McCreedy. Oh, she was being ridiculous! She accelerated sharply. She knew full well that the dressmaker had not had a fair deal out of life: she had been abandoned, obliged to struggle for her living, bring up a child and bear all her worries alone. At the time when she herself might have had to accept such a fate it had seemed like the end of the world; she had panicked. Nowadays, people thought less of such things, though in the Braids district illegitimate births were still not looked on with much favour.

But she no longer knew what was fair or unfair. She knew very little, she realised, as she braked at the lights and almost ran into the back of a double-decker bus. The incident did not unnerve her as it normally would have done; she sat with composure waiting for the lights to change and the back end of the bus to part company with her bumper.

As she approached the Church Hill Theatre she remembered Conal McCreedy, and there was the sign up: *The Caledonian Players* in *Long Day's Journey Into Night*. Now she knew what she would do this evening.

Chapter Two

THE auditorium was half full, the producer reported, after he had taken a quick look round the side of the curtain, and that, even though part of it was 'paper', was not bad, considering it was the first night and the play was one which might not appeal to too many people. Also, it was frightfully long in spite of their having made a few cuts, which in itself had been difficult with Conal McCreedy resisting every attempt to shorten his own lengthy speeches. McCreedy, who was making himself up in front of the mirror, did not flicker an eyelash at the remarks. They had been through all this before, during the choosing of the play, and the producer had gone on about the dreariness of O'Neill and folk wanting to come out for an evening and be entertained rather than be sent home thinking suicide would be a good way out. McCreedy had got his way, as usual, as he did in the six other drama groups he belonged to around the city. No one could remember when anyone else had last chosen a play. The producer, who dressed the windows in a Princes Street store during the day, resolved that next time it was going to be Noël Coward or Alan Ayckbourne or he would leave and form his own group.

'Five minutes,' called the stage manager, setting up a chorus of protests.

In the third row sat Emily Mountjoy, hands folded on her lap, eyes fixed on the curtain waiting for it to open and reveal Conal. Unexpectedly, she did not feel in the least bit odd at being on her own despite the fact that most of the audience seemed to be in groups and know one another well. There was a great deal of waving going on. Relatives and friends, she supposed, come to give their support. There was no sign of Conal's only relation.

On her right-hand side sat another woman who seemed also to be alone. She had long slim hands which Emily Mountjoy envied

25

and between them she held a copy of the play. It was much marked and annotated. She herself knew nothing of the play, except that she had a vague notion it was about O'Neill's own family, and was content to sit with her ignorance, ready to accept the new experience as it came. Her head was light and she had a feeling that she might be humming to herself from time to time though could not be sure. After passing the theatre earlier she had driven down to the George Hotel where she had spent the intervening time drinking martinis and pretending to read the *Scottish Field*. Her only food had been a few salted peanuts and a bar of chocolate purchased from a slot machine.

'They're late,' said her right-hand neighbour, revealing at once which part of the world she came from.

Emily Mountjoy nodded and smiled, not caring how late they were. She had all the time in the world.

The house grew a little restless, someone began to sing, 'Oh, why are we waiting', but was hushed immediately, and then, ten minutes after the hour appointed, the lights dimmed, somebody dropped something in the wings, and the curtain opened. Emily Mountjoy leaned forward, allowing herself to be drawn straight in to the shabby living room of James Tyrone's summer house on a morning in August 1912. It was going to be painful, she sensed that at once, in spite of the affectionate enough opening between husband and wife (she could not imagine Farquhar putting his arm round her and saying she was a fine armful!); the people in this family were going to torment themselves and one another, they were going to expose their hate and love, guilt and despair; they were going to accuse, to rip away all the outer protective devices. Her daughter was the only one in her family who did any overt accusing but hers was mild and postured compared with this. In her family they sat on their despair.

Conal became James Tyrone, in every gesture, word, movement. He had the measure of all the characters; he led them, drew from them, enhanced them.

Most times in recent years when she had been to the theatre — they tended to go to Shakespeare or Chekhov at the Festival — she had found the experience to be one of sitting back and viewing with detachment. This, however, was different: she felt sucked in, she identified with each and every one of the characters. Strange, when all but one were so hammily played. And considering that she had had no close involvement with drug addiction, alcoholism, or wasting diseases. But there were many moments of recognition for her, many echoes that she caught, responded to, recognising the validity of their truth. *None of us can help the things life has done to us. They're done before you realise it, and once they're done they make you do other things until at last everything comes between you and what you'd like to be, and you've lost your true self forever.* She did not quite believe that one could not help the things one did but vibrated fully to the proposition that they were done before one realised it. Was she speaking aloud? She felt that her lips were moving. No one was looking at her. Everyone was watching the stage. Everyone was watching Conal McCreedy.

At the end of Act Two the applause was loud.

Emily Mountjoy and her neighbour did not join the scramble for coffee and orange juice. 'Pity there's no bar,' said the American, but Emily Mountjoy did not mind. She wanted to sit where she was and reflect on what she had seen and heard. She thought of Mary Tyrone's last words when she had been left alone talking to herself at the end of the act, her husband and sons having just gone out.

Their contempt and disgust aren't pleasant company. You're glad they've gone. Then Mother of God, why do I feel so lonely?

'He's fantastic, that guy. What's his name again?'

'Conal McCreedy.' She was pleased to have the opportunity to say it aloud.

'You've seen him before?'

'Not on the stage.'

'You know him then? Off stage?'

She nodded and smiled.

'I must say he's giving a marvellous interpretation of Tyrone senior. The rest are all shit. He ought to go on the stage proper. Instead of messing around with a bunch of amateurs.'

'Oh, but he's not an amateur.' She felt quite shocked by the suggestion. 'At least, I don't believe he is.' Now that she came to think of it she was not at all clear. Conal was an actor. Mrs Seton always referred to him as one. Did it matter whether he was classed as an amateur or a professional?

'I would imagine so, to him. He won't get paid for this, you know. What does he do for a living?'

She confessed that she did not know and then revealed the extent of her knowledge concerning him.

'So his mother's a dressmaker? That's interesting. I could use a new dress or two.'

She looked as if she could easily buy off the peg, having no problems about overgenerous endowment, but Emily Mountjoy did not say so. The lights were dimming again.

When the final curtain came down the applause that rang out was primarily for Conal McCreedy, of that she felt sure. Without him the play would have foundered. She watched him as he held hands with the others, bowed, with grave expression, not showing any of the exultation he must have felt. After several curtain calls, the clapping died away and the curtain cut off the players from the audience. She was left with the image of Conal's face before her eyes, and Mary Tyrone's last words washing through her head.

Then in the spring something happened to me. Yes, I remember. I fell in love with James Tyrone and was happy for a time.

For a time . . .

'I sure as heck wouldn't have liked to endure the inward agony that lay behind the writing of that play.'

'But what if one endures inward agony and creates no play?'

The American was eyeing her with surprise. 'You don't suffer agony, do you? I don't believe it.'

'Why not?'

'You look –'

'Too comfortable? Just because of this too solid flesh?'

No, no! Her neighbour's protests were emphatic and accompanied with embarrassed laughter. Emily Mountjoy laughed too. Her agony was allowed to go, and they agreed that it was a powerful play. The American had made a special study of O'Neill for her master's degree and that was how she had come to be here tonight. 'I came out of curiosity to see what they'd make of it. And, you know, I'd sure like to have a word with this Conal

What's-his-name? You wouldn't care to introduce me, would you?'

Why not? Emily Mountjoy still felt gay; de-intoxication had not yet set in. She felt badly a few hours after drink, usually went into a trough of depression. As yet, she was reprieved.

'Say, what's your name? Mine's Louisa Grant. Yes, you're right – Scots' ancestors and I do intend to try track them down – and my mother was mad on *Jo's Boys*.'

In response to that she could merely say, 'Emily Mountjoy,' without qualification.

'Mountjoy? That's not a Scots name, is it? Sounds more like Irish.'

Emily could not disagree. Her husband's family seemed to have acquired their name by some kind of freak accident. His ancestors had inhabited the city of Edinburgh for several generations, practised law and medicine within its confines, and been involved in its politics; and he resented greatly any suggestion that he might be Irish. He had sometimes been tempted to remove the 'joy' and make it into a more dignified name. At times too he had been embarrassed by it and on one occasion an I.R.A. sympathiser had approached him, assuming that his sympathies must lie in the same direction as his own. To have a name linking you with Ireland's great! He had started blathering on about McCracken and Pearse and Connolly. Afterwards Farquhar had had a quiet word with the police.

None of this information did his wife impart to her new acquaintance as they made their way up the aisle together.

It was only as they were entering the stage door that she began to regret her impulsiveness. What if Conal did not recognise her? A girl in jeans, sensing her hesitation, accosted them.

'We're looking for Conal McCreedy,' said Louisa.

The dressing room was full to overflowing and smelled of sweat and make-up. Relatives and friends were exploding with superlatives.

Conal was leaning against the wall smoking a cigarette.

'Friends here for you, Conal.'

The hot flush was going to come back, she could feel it threatening, and fought to keep it down. The room was so hot she thought she might faint.

And then she saw him coming towards them, pushing his way through the bodies and he was smiling, saying, 'How kind of you to come! Of course I remember you! You were at my mother's this afternoon.'

The flush receded. She took his hand and he pressed hers, firmly. 'You were marvellous,' she gasped.

Some half an hour later she found herself drinking Guinness in *Bennet's Bar* at Tollcross. The pub was genuine Victorian with stained glass and mirrors and heavily carved woodwork. Not that one could make out much of the detail through the fog of cigarette smoke and conglomeration of pressing bodies, though she was doing her best to. She and Farquhar did not frequent public houses. It was all Louisa's doing, of course, that they were here. Conal had been amazingly compliant, and later confessed that he had been glad of an excuse to get away from his fellow players. Also, he liked the unexpected. And Louisa and Mrs Mountjoy had been unexpected.

Standing up, Emily Mountjoy drank her Guinness, raising her glass to her mouth with some difficulty due to the lack of space but feeling no irritation, and whenever an elbow jogged her and some of the dark brown liquid trickled up her sleeve she merely laughed. The noise was hectic and unrelenting. She remembered the hushed silence in her thick house. She smiled at everyone who looked her way. Louisa talked to Conal about O'Neill, talked earnestly in the way that Americans did, not giving in to the crush and noise, and when someone pushed past she swayed and rallied to re-put her point about the Jungian influences in the playwright's work. Emily Mountjoy felt bewitched by her intelligence and energy. Straining to listen, she caught through the confusion of sound such words and phrases as tension and conflict, significance of pain, individuation. 'I do believe it is only through constant struggle and change that we really come to the full realization of our inner personality, don't you?'

Conal, who had his ear inclined, nodded. Constant change, repeated Emily aloud, unheard. If what Louisa said was true then

Emily felt her own inner personality must be about the size of a pea.

'Let's get out of here,' said Louisa after a while. Her voice had begun to hoarsen. 'Let's go to my place.'

They followed her out, like lambs, agreeable to be led. The night air was cool after the heat of the pub. Emily Mountjoy put up the collar of her beaver.

'You've lost your hat,' said Louisa.

She put a hand to her head. So she had! Not to worry about a trifle like that. They went for her car, Conal walking between them, linking arms.

'Say that line for me again, would you, Conal?' she asked. 'The bit about the days of wine and roses.'

' "They are not long, the days of wine and roses",' he said softly.

And Louisa continued:

' "Out of a misty dream
   Our path emerges for a while, then closes." '

' "Within a dream",' finished Conal.

Within a dream, repeated Emily to herself, as she drove to Louisa's place which turned out to be a bed-sitter at Newington, a pretty dreadful bed-sitter of the kind that Emily had not laid eyes on for years and did not appear to have changed much during that time: the overwhelming mood was of porridge and yellow varnish, and the room was in one of those large houses that had a red neon sign above the front door saying *Guest House* and a garden that had been torn up to make a car park for three cars.

They sat in front of a one-bar electric fire and drank instant coffee from cups that were frazzled with grey cracks.

'It's a dreadful place, isn't it? I can't wait to get out of it. Edinburgh's full of such gorgeous property I feel it's a crying shame to live in a dump like this.'

Mrs Mountjoy – or Emily, as they insisted on calling her – told her then about the McCreedy's flat. It was just the kind of place that Louisa would adore to have, old, steeped in history, and non-suburban.

'I hate the suburbs.'

'I live in a suburb,' said Emily mournfully.

Louisa said that she was sure Emily would have put her own special stamp on her home and she had no need to sound apologetic, and she, Louisa, would love to visit her there. They exchanged telephone numbers.

'I must say I am not fond of the suburbs either,' said Conal. He had lived all his life in the heart of the city and could not conceive of living anywhere else. Whenever he went on a journey, however small, he saw himself as passing through rings of time: he emerged from the centre, from the medieval old town, to traverse the streets of Georgian elegance, and then came the Victorian villas – here Emily nodded – and after them the bungalows, of the twenties and thirties, and now of the sixties and seventies, forming estates, communities that meant nothing at all to him; and finally, on the very outer limits of the city, in the edges of wasteland, stood the tall grey blocks like sentinels on guard. In these high slabs lived people plucked from the city's heart, from the Grassmarket and Canongate, Lawnmarket and Cowgate, and out of them the gangs emerged, booted, afraid, carrying knives, creating havoc, leaving their slogans around the city, on doors, walls, shops, in Lover's Loan. Young terrors. His mother used to call him a holy terror but she had not meant he carried a knife and a spray can.

Emily sat back, bemused by his flow of words, by the excellence of his delivery. Since after lunch she had been bemused by a succession of people and events.

'Not all who live in wasteland are terrors,' Louisa reminded him.

'You are right, Louisa. Lou-i-sa. We're off to Louisiana in the morning,' he sang.

'I'm from Chicago, well, sort of.'

'Plenty of terrors there, so we hear,' he said, relapsing into indolence, lying back in the grubby moquette armchair so elegantly that it was possible to believe he reclined on a chaise longue. He appeared to veer between two moods, the one indolent, the other passionate and eloquent. Emily felt that she should have been asking questions about the Black Problem and urban violence but was too somnolent to bother. She thought she must be swaying slightly, from the waist up. Louisa was the only one with any

32

energy left, and hers seemed to stem from some limitless store.

'The pot of oil that never runs dry,' murmured Emily.

'There's no oil in Chicago, Emily. You're thinking of Dallas.'

But she was not really thinking about anything. Her mind was as near to being blank as it had ever been. Odd words and phrases drifted through it like bits of dreams that were unconnected; she made no attempt to snatch them, hold them back, order them. She felt as if she was floating on a cloud, a pink one, edged with gold, like the wicker chair she sat upon. Louisa began to explain how she was not exactly from Chicago, having been born in Philadelphia, though had left there when she was three weeks old and naturally therefore could not feel she was a Philadelphian. You had to say you were from somewhere when you were asked and since she had spent four years at university in Chicago, which was the longest time she had spent anywhere, that seemed as good an answer as any. Her listeners' attention sharpened. They had both spent the last thirty years or so of their lives in the same house, never mind the same city. They looked at one another, then back at Louisa. She was saying that she had moved twenty-seven times before she was eighteen. 'How exhausting,' said Conal, yawning, sliding lower into his chair. Exciting, suggested Emily, throwing in the word. At times it had been, Louisa admitted; every time she and her father had packed up she had felt a tide of exhilaration coursing through her system and she had thought that this time would be it. 'It?' asked Conal. 'Something miraculous, I suppose. I guess I was always hoping for a miracle.' She laughed. 'But usually it was a case of the same old clapped-out boarding house full of clapped-out people. The walls were always thin and you could hear them shouting or crying behind them at night.' Emily and Conal stared with astonishment at this vision of alien life. And here was Louisa now in another boarding house – if not clapped-out then at least it must be called unexciting and lacking in anything miraculous – but without her father. Presumably he was back in the States, somewhere. It seemed pointless to ask where.

'Where was your mother?' asked Emily, suddenly realising that some element was missing from the narrative.

'Oh, she took off when I was three years old.'

'Abandoned you?'

'Went off with another guy.'

Conal sat up. 'My father left *before* I was born.'

'That must have been tough.'

'On his mother,' said Emily.

Her own childhood appeared extraordinarily ordinary set against their experiences. She had been born in a house in Colinton, lived there until she left to marry Farquhar Mountjoy (the reception was held in a marquee on the lawn) and had a sister and a brother, and neither her mother nor father had ever contemplated abandoning each other, as far as she knew. They had died within a year of each other, were buried in the same grave.

'Oh, some Americans live that way too, you know. They're not all like me.'

'The boarding houses would be full if they were,' said Conal.

'A little bit of movement might be a good thing though,' said Emily.

But why had she and her father kept moving all the time? Louisa said he had been a frustrated architect; he had qualified as a draftsman, was always moving from job to job, choosing the location first because of some architect who worked or had worked there. Thus they went in and out of New York, never staying long because the city created too many problems; they went to Arizona and Chicago to see the work of Frank Lloyd Wright, to Pasadena to see the work of the Greene brothers, to Oklahoma to see the work of Bruce Goff. Other times, there were other excuses. Most times they moved they changed states. And that was her life until she was eighteen. Then she became a student, was forced to be static for a while, and it was during that time that she entered into her first marriage.

'First?' said Emily.

'Four in all. Chicago, Illinois. Tombstone, Arizona. Seattle, Washington. Boston, Massachusetts.' She might have been chanting a litany. 'They were all lawyers, or law students.'

'My husband's a lawyer. He's a Writer to Her Majesty's Signet. It's a most august club, the holiest of the holy, if you happen to be a Scottish lawyer.' It was the first time since leaving home that

34

Emily had thought of Farquhar. At once she allowed him to glide back into the shadows, murmuring vaguely when Louisa said she would love to meet him. She felt absorbed by Louisa's life. She waited, knowing there must be more to come, for the American, sitting on the edge of her high-backed chair, looked charged with energy. They listened attentively, she and Conal, to details of marriages and divorces, changing of jobs, packing up, travelling for three days at a stretch to reach the new rooming house, all momentous life upheavals for most people – for them, even as a concept – and yet Louisa had done each thing so often that they were inclined to think she must have lived several lives simultaneously.

'And now you are in Scotland,' said Conal.

'That's because of my interest in fortified houses and castles. Oh, that's not the official reason, but that's the real reason. I first became obsessed with the idea of the fortified house when I was about seven years old. We were living in the mid-west, it was hot and humid, and we were sitting on the porch getting bitten to death by mosquitoes. Pa had just been to the library, he'd brought back this book on castles and fortified houses in Scotland. He opened it up and we began to look at it together and he told me stories about the people who'd lived in the castles. He was great at making up stories. And it looked so cool and private inside those thick stone buildings. That was me hooked. We moved before we could return the book, so we took it with us. I longed for a house made of thick thick stone with narrow slitted windows, an impregnable, impenetrable house. No doubt the psychiatrists would have plenty to say about that. Oh yes, have had plenty!'

'So you always knew you would come to Scotland one day to pursue your obsession?' said Conal.

'Right.'

'And what is your official reason for coming to Scotland?'

She told them she had got some money to do research for a book on American Women in Scotland. Would there be much interest in that? asked Emily. 'There's a lot of interest in Scotland in America,' said Louisa. 'And there *are* a lot of American women.' It had been a good excuse for her to come over, which was all she had been waiting for. Emily was interested. Which American women were they that Louisa had in mind? They must be well known, she presumed, or have done something? 'There's Harriet Beecher Stowe for a start,' said Louisa. 'Oh God,' said Conal. 'Sunny Memories of the Highlands of Scotland. What a nerve she had! Ten-day coach tour. I record only the sunny hours. Scotland was bleeding at the time, its cottages newly cleared, roofs ripped off, burnt, people evicted.' Louisa agreed that she was none too fond of Mrs Beecher Stowe but she would be obliged to include her. A little controversy was always welcome. Who else? Emily wanted to know. Louisa mentioned the novelist Edith Wharton. Born and bred in old New York, she later forsook America for France.

'And Scotland?'

'Not exactly. She did come here though for a tour in September 1934, when she was seventy-two years old.'

'Oh,' said Emily. To her it did not sound too promising but then she was inexperienced in this area of life, as in many others. 'Can you make much of all that?'

'Something. Which is all I need to do.'

'I remember Mary McCarthy was here, summer of '62,' said Emily suddenly. She had come to a novelists' conference in the McEwen Hall. 'All sorts of interesting people came – Lawrence Durrell, Muriel Spark, Nathalie Sarraute, Henry Miller, Alberto Moravio, and I remember Norman Mailer flying in late – his wife, at that time, had just had a baby girl. What excitement we had that week! Imagine all those interesting people coming to Edinburgh at the same time! I went to every session, enjoyed it all immensely. Nothing quite like it has ever happened in Edinburgh since, not in a literary way.'

'To return to Mary McCarthy,' said Louisa, 'I can't use her. The women have to be dead. Too many problems if they're not.' But Emily was worried that there would not be enough women for Louisa. Couldn't they invent some? suggested Conal. They could have a lot of fun and nobody would be any the wiser. But Louisa was confident she would be able to dig up some minor figures, and they could – if they would like to – help, and anyway, the main thing was that she was here, and there was no shortage of fortified houses and castles. She would love to help, cried Emily;

36

with the American women, not so much the castles, though she was willing to go on visits to them too. Tonight she felt ready for anything.

'So now you know all about me.' Louisa settled her bottom against the back of her chair and looked at them, implying it was their turn. They looked at the orange coil of heat. It seemed to be pulsating slightly. 'What do you do, Conal?'

'I act.' He unfolded his hands. Ah yes, but that was not what Louisa meant. What did he do for a living? Emily felt shocked that she should ask the question so directly. 'This and that.' He shrugged. 'A bit of modelling, some television work occasionally.' But not as a paid-up member of Equity? persisted Louisa. She could have terrier-like qualities, thought Emily; teeth into the bone and hang on tight. No, he was not a member of Equity, he admitted, pulling back the sleeve of his blue velvet jacket. He remarked on the lateness of the hour, adding that his mother would be waiting up for him. For a moment Emily thought Louisa was about to make a further remark, but then the girl thought better of it and closed her mouth tightly like one who had decided to contain herself against all her instincts, at least for the moment.

Emily offered Conal a lift home, and Louisa waved them off from the doorstep, standing under the neon sign, crying out to them to take care and she would see them both again soon. With a certain feeling of panache, Emily drove to the Grassmarket. Conal remained unperturbed, even when she went through a red light. There was not much traffic about anyway. Coming down Candlemaker Row into the Grassmarket, she glanced up ahead and saw a light shining out like a beacon from the top flat. The star in the North. She swerved, turned her eyes back to the road again. Her passenger seemed to have nerves as relaxed as a sleeping kitten's.

She drew round in a wide flourish to brake outside the Mc-Creedy's door. Conal appeared to be in no hurry to alight. He lit a cigarette and for the length of time it took to smoke it he talked to her about Arthur Miller, the next playwright whose work he was to appear in. He was to play Willy Loman in *Death of a Salesman*. She would not have minded what he spoke of, she

37

enjoyed the sound of his voice so much; it rose and fell like the waves of the sea and at one point she lost all track of his discourse and was wafted off into a floating dream. Then her head jerked forward and she became aware again of his words. He was saying something about Willy Loman achieving the ultimate in salesmanship by selling the American dream to himself.

'And then there's Louisa's father. I suppose he must have been searching for a dream in all that wandering about.'

'They certainly lived mobile lives,' murmured Emily.

'Unlike us, eh? We are static people, Emily, you and I.'

For a moment she was silent and then she cried out, 'But we don't have to be!' surprising herself by the forcefulness of her feeling. 'I believe in change, Conal. Yes, I do!' 'Free will?' Maybe not entirely free, but she did not believe in predetermination either, she refused to. He did not say what he believed in, she only realised afterwards.

He rolled down the window and tossed out the cigarette end. It was time for him to go. She wished he would ask her to go with him and then they might sit, all three, up there, before the fire, and continue talking about dreams and the possibility of change; but of course that was too much to expect. He got out of the car, came round to the driver's side and taking her hand between both of his, kissed the back, sending ripples of pleasure which ran right up her arm to her neck.

And then he was gone. The pavement was empty. She blinked, wondering if she had imagined him, but his smell was still inside the car and she knew that he had been real enough. All her senses were alive, sharp, receiving. She caressed the hand he had kissed with her other one. It was the first time a man had ever kissed her hand. It was not a Scottish custom. Conal, she fancied, would have most of the qualities she had been brought up not to admire in a man. She had grown up expecting a man to behave like Farquhar.

She could imagine what her friend Mrs Seton would say about her evening. Mrs Seton moved only within prescribed limits, keeping close rein on her mind, letting nothing in that might disturb the status quo. And that brought her back to thoughts of Camilla. She frowned, not wishing to think in Camilla's jargon, but soon she smiled again for she felt in such good humour with the night that nothing could disturb her for more than a passing second. She was tempted to go for an excursion through the city, to leave the car and go on foot down the length of the Royal Mile as far as the gates of Holyrood Palace, dawdling a little here and there to peer into the mouth of a dark close, or stare at a lit window, imagining the people beyond and linking herself with them. She felt a part of all the people in the city tonight, those who slept, those who were awake, talking, laughing, giving birth, dying. She shivered.

A dark figure was tapping on her window. She wound it down.

'Anything the matter, madam?'

'Oh, nothing, thank you, constable. I was just having a little rest.'

Driving away, she was conscious of his eyes watching her for the length of the Grassmarket. She felt possessed of unusual insight tonight, which allowed her to sense what everyone else was doing or thinking. She knew too that it would be a mistake to take her solitary walk; it would be tempting fate too far, and she had had pleasure enough for one day. Not that it was still the same day. She had made her own day's journey into night and it had been neither long nor agonising.

All the lights were on in her house on the Braids Hill when she arrived; they streamed out from uncurtained windows making patterns of light and dark across the front lawn. And in the street stood two empty police cars nose to tail as if they had been driven at speed and stopped abruptly. She passed them, turning into the drive, glancing the side of the car off the gatepost, and was delighted to get into the space left in the garage between her husband's Rover and her son's abandoned M.G.

She emerged from the garage humming.

Farquhar was standing on the front doorstep.

'Emily, for Christ's sake!'

Startled, she took a step back. It was so unlike Farquhar to swear. 'What is it, dear?' she said.

'Do you realise – ' he swallowed ' – what time it is?'

'Not exactly. Late, I suppose.'

But not too late. Earlier that day she had been thinking that it was.

Three other men, two in plain clothes, and one in uniform, had appeared behind Farquhar in the porch. He came down the steps.

'The house has been burgled, all our valuables taken. They got in through the drawing-room window which someone had left unsnibbed. Your car was missing from the garage and so were you. We thought you might have been kidnapped.'

'Kidnapped?' She began to laugh.

'It has been known to happen, madam, unfortunately,' said one of the plain-clothes men. 'We thought the thieves could have forced you to drive them away.'

She knew her irresistible desire to laugh was not going to help matters, to smooth the furrowed brows and straighten the pursed lips, but she could not restrain it.

Chapter Three

'You don't even seem to appreciate what I went through!'

Emily Mountjoy, sipping weak tea in an effort to quench her thirst and drown her headache, tried to sympathise, to show understanding, but by the look in her husband's exasperated eye knew she was failing. She had been thinking about Conal's performance as James Tyrone. She would have preferred to stay in bed that morning and mull it over, as well as their conversation in the car in the middle of the night, but having no wish to add to Farquhar's irritation had struggled up, fighting back waves of nausea, to make his porridge and kippers. The fish had been a real test of self-control. Before the whole cholesterol thing had taken on and it became taboo to eat more than two eggs a week Farquhar used to have bacon and a fried egg every morning. All her married life she had struggled not to exasperate her husband, to tone herself down, though often had been at a loss to know why it was exactly that she was irritating him. Merely by being herself, she presumed. Camilla said she was a coward, bought by money, comfort, etc. Most of Camilla's pronouncements could be put in the form of etceteras. She had been here last night awaiting her mother's return, having been summoned from Stockbridge by her father. She had been sitting on the couch wearing a striped jumper of so many colours that Joseph's coat would have been put to shame.

'I thought you'd run away from home. Good for you, I thought, not before time. But I might have known.' She had not waited to hear where it was that her mother had been but jumped on her bicycle, which had no lights, as the uniformed policeman was quick to point out, and pedalled off back to Carl who would be wondering where the hell *she* had got to by this time.

No, better not to think of Camilla. Better to think of Conal McCreedy.

'What *are* you smiling about, Emily?' Farquhar pushed aside his porridge, half-eaten, out of which stuck up a few grey lumps like slag heaps.

'Nothing, dear.'

'I shouldn't think you'd anything to smile about. Not after last night. You made a real fool out of me, you know.'

'I'm sorry, Farquhar.' She had repeated the phrase last night after the policemen went, many times, like a record stuck in a groove, and had realised that she had not meant it, not in the slightest. And she did not mean it now either, which was even more strange, for although de-intoxication was well under way repentance was not.

Farquhar got up, thrusting his chair aside, and inadvertently crumpled his *Scotsman* which he liked to be kept clean and un-creased. He ran his hand up the back of his head, and for a moment she saw the young man in him, the one she had married in St Giles with a stream of bridesmaids behind her looking like sweet peas. It had been a happy day. She remembered the feeling of having landed safely on the shore. Those days did appear to have been more serene on the whole, seen in retrospect. Things might not have been perfect (there was, after all, the Bomb, and all that) but one knew where one stood and there was less confusion around.

'Are you sure you're all right, Emily?'

'I'm fine, Farquhar, really.'

'You don't think you should see old Sutherland, get some more pills?'

'I've got enough pills.'

'Or even see a –'

He let it go, telling her to take it easy, and why not have a morning in town, buy herself a new hat, and perhaps meet a friend for lunch? He would have taken her for a run down the coast himself but had a busy morning ahead, offers were closing for a big property over Ravelston way at twelve noon.

'Another high noon for you, eh, Farquhar?' Quickly she added, 'No, no, truly, I *am* fine.'

At last he went. He had forgotten to eat his kippers. And they were so expensive nowadays, with the herring crisis.

42

Louisa rang mid-morning and Emily invited her to lunch. She prepared some chicken mayonnaise and salad and put a bottle of white Moselle wine in the fridge to chill. By the time Louisa arrived her headache had quite gone.

For the first time she had a proper look at her new friend. Last night she had received only an impression of the girl, and it was as a girl she categorised her in her mind although she must be something over thirty years old. How far over she could not tell for she found that the older she got the more difficult it was for her to guess the age of anyone younger than herself. Older people were easier; liver spots and receding gums were dead giveaways. She hated the sight of her own lengthening teeth. Louisa's were in perfect shape and she herself was as slim as a bamboo reed, with skin that matched in colour (due to hot summers in the mid-west, no doubt), and she wore steel-rimmed glasses that framed very large and searching grey eyes.

'I'm far too skinny, I know. I can't seem to put on any weight.'

'Put the two of us together, cut us in half, and we might average out to one normal person.' Emily laughed.

She found that she could say whatever came into her head to Louisa, and, what was more amazing, talk intimately with her. It was years since she had talked intimately to anyone, not since the days of having children when one launched easily into conversations about contraception and breast-feeding with other women in a similar position on short acquaintanceship.

'I suppose you would say I am at a point in my life when I need to make a change, Louisa. I feel a bit like a tent that has been anchored down all these years and now its guy-ropes have been unpegged and I am in danger of blowing away. If I was slightly younger – or perhaps even just slightly slimmer! – I might have an affair. But I think that would hardly do for me.' She had had a long look at herself naked before the mirror that morning and knew that it would not. The idea even of a strange man seeing her flabby, veined flesh had given her the shudders. 'Besides, sex no longer interests me.'

'Has it ever?'

'Once. Not for a long time.'

'It might start to again. If you met the right man.'

'Come now, Louisa, you're not going to give me a little talk about Mr Right!' She was enjoying herself thoroughly. Talking about sex in relation to herself! Whatever next? They had finished the wine which had disappeared remarkably quickly. She decided they could do with another bottle and went to fetch one from the cupboard under the stairs where Farquhar kept his wine stock. He was no layer down of wine cellars, bought only a bottle or two at a time. Fortunately there was a second bottle of the Moselle.

'I wouldn't dream of advising you to seek salvation through a man, Emily,' said Louisa, when she returned. 'It's not on. I know that only too well.'

Emily put the bottle between her feet and screwed in the opener. The cork came up sharply. 'Four times married is quite a lot.'

'You could say I'm a sucker for a challenge, eh?'

Emily would drink to that. There were worse things one could be in life. One could be too cautious: she knew that. Louisa thought she needed another interest, a part-time job, old hat as that suggestion might be; but what could she do? Emily asked, for she had never had a job in her life, which was a dreadful thing for a woman to have to confess to these days. She had married straight after graduation. Yes, she had graduated. 'Only an ordinary M.A., mind you, but at least it was something.' Not that it had ever been of any practical use to her. Of course one should not expect education always to be that. But what could she do now? She waited, confidently, for Louisa to come up with some suggestion.

When the second bottle was drained they had come to a few decisions. Emily was to begin on a weight-reducing programme, on grounds of health alone, not in order to please or attract a man, change her hairstyle, simply for the boost it would give to her morale, take up Yoga, to rejuvenate and invigorate her system, start systematically to read and reread all the books she'd been meaning to for years, and help Louisa with her research on American women in Scotland. Louisa was not so daft as to suggest that she dress herself in kaftans and ropes of beads or leave her husband, as Camilla would have done.

'Along the way other possibilities are bound to crop up.' And now Louisa wanted something of Emily: an introduction to Mrs McCreedy.

The dressmaker had a customer in for a fitting. As they stood at the door trying to talk their way in they could hear her hoarse catarrhal cough coming from the inner room. Mrs Mountjoy was apologetic for calling without warning, but Louisa smiled and spoke enthusiastically of the dressmaker's reputation and they were admitted. They were asked if they would mind waiting in Conal's room as it was the only other one the flat possessed apart from the kitchenette and bathroom.

Conal was not there, of course, being in the Borders filming *Kenilworth*. It was raining outside, would probably be wet and muddy for him underfoot, observed Emily. Louisa was already examining his room, her head poked forward on the thin stalk of its neck. There were more pictures of himself and his productions on the walls, prints of Van Gogh, Raoul Dufy and Matisse, and three small oil paintings by nineteenth-century Scottish painters. Around the room he had several pieces of Art Nouveau, including a cabinet with interesting glass. 'He's spent quite a bit of bread on this lot,' murmured Louisa. 'Or somebody has.' The two women browsed happily, Emily with a vague but subdued sense of guilt at looking at someone else's property without his permission, although Louisa seemed to feel no inhibitions whatsoever and even opened a drawer to look inside.

And then the other customer was heard leaving, after asking that Mrs McCreedy should convey her regards to Conal, and they were called in.

Louisa removed her jeans and sweater without a flicker of hesitation and stood before the fire, semi-naked. Flicking her inch-tape, Mrs McCreedy shook her head at the angular jutting bones; and from her place on the chaise longue Emily looked on in wonder and prodded her own hip to see if she could locate the bone underneath.

'You need a bit beef on those bones, lass.'

'Perhaps I should fill up with some of your good old Scots porridge and oatcakes.'

Mrs McCreedy, who never ate either, made no comment.

She wrote down the numbers in her notebook and saw that in some cases they were almost half the size of Mrs Mountjoy's which were on the adjacent page.

Louisa, body held still but eyes roving, admired the room in all its aspects, and when released from the bond of the inchtape went to the window which she pushed up so that she could look down on the view and praise that also. She was unruffled when the dressmaker pointed out that she could be seen in her brassière from the street below. 'They're welcome to look, as long as they don't touch. At least not without permission! Difficult to do from down there, eh? They'd need long fingers.' Mrs Mountjoy laughed but Mrs McCreedy was not amused. She gave Louisa a long look through the thick glass of her spectacles. She was not keen on Americans and seldom took one as a customer but had allowed herself to be swayed this time because she was a friend of Mrs Mountjoy and Mrs Mountjoy was a friend of Mrs Seton. And here she was regretting it already, instinctively. Her judgments of people were all made on instinct. The American was too angular, too probing, too penetrating. Such sharpness grated on her senses, made her want to draw back, keep her distance. But it was difficult to keep at a distance when one must go close to a physical body, touch the flesh, feel the other person's breath on one's neck, kneel before her.

'Do you know, it's like being in a fortified house up here? The walls are thick and it's high . . . It feels impregnable!' Louisa laughed and the sound sailed out of the window so that they only caught the edge of it against the roar of the traffic below. Emily told Mrs McCreedy about Louisa's obsession, not using the word itself, but substituting 'interest', which she felt would be more acceptable to the dressmaker.

'I'd just adore to live in a fortified house, Mrs McCreedy,' said Louisa, turning back into the room. 'It's one of my dreams.'

Mrs McCreedy would not think of asking what the others were. She closed her notebook, laid it on the mantelpiece below the crucified Christ, and stuck her pencil behind her ear. Louisa began now to talk about the Grassmarket and its history. 'Pretty bloody history it was too, wasn't it?' She had been to see the grave of Captain Porteous who had been lynched by the mob bent on

46

taking justice into their own hands. She had been busy since she'd come to Edinburgh, commented Mrs McCreedy. And then there were the Covenanters, said Louisa. She admired people who took a stand for their beliefs and were prepared even to die for them.

'Nothing's worth getting hung on the gibbet for, if you ask me,' said Mrs McCreedy, taking the inchtape from around her neck and winding it tightly round the forefinger of her left hand.

'Is there nothing you'd be prepared to die for, Mrs McCreedy?'

'I don't know about you ladies but I've got better things to do than talk about dying.'

At once Mrs Mountjoy was up and on her feet. Louisa moved more slowly, taking time about the replacing of her garments.

On the way down the stairs they passed an amply built lady in a fur coat. They did not speak.

From there Louisa took Emily to a hairdresser's, again talking themselves in without an appointment and Emily had her hair cut and blown dry. All traces of her previous bouffant style were removed. She emerged with a much sleeker head. She looked ten years younger, declared Louisa.

It was then five o'clock.

'Opening time,' said Louisa.

She might only have been in Edinburgh for three months but her knowledge of the city was remarkable, observed Emily, as they stood at the *Abbotsford*'s mahogany carved bar in Rose Street drinking malt whisky. This was a very obvious pub – Louisa spoke dismissively – but she would take Emily to a few less-well-known ones where people other than poets and B.B.C. men hung around. She knew one or two in Leith that they might visit. There were a great many things they might do.

'There are indeed,' said Emily.

After a couple of drinks she took Louisa home and then returned to her villa. The telephone was ringing as she unlocked the three locks on the front door.

'Where the hell have you been?' demanded Farquhar. She smiled into the hall mirror. If she was not in her place he himself felt disorientated. Sometimes people had to learn to reorientate themselves. 'Emily, are you saying something? I've been ringing

47

all afternoon! I'd expected to be home by now but I've got caught up –'

Not wishing to hear in what, she jumped in to say that he should not worry, she was perfectly all right and did not mind if he was not in for dinner.

For several seconds there was silence. She was about to say goodbye when he said, 'You are remembering the Jamieson-Browns are coming for dinner this evening? And Davina and Elspeth? At seven-thirty?'

Now she was silent. She eased her wrist from under its beaver covering and saw that her watch said a quarter to seven.

'You've forgotten, haven't you, Emily?'

She denied it. Everything was under control, she told him, and he should calm down. He would be back by seven-fifteen, he said, making it sound like a threat – not that he had ever threatened her in his life – and put down the receiver.

The first thing was not to panic, although strangely, she felt no inclination to. It was too late to take anything out of the deep freeze except perhaps mince but she could scarcely offer hamburgers. Then she had a brainwave. She took the car out again and drove to the nearest fish-and-chip shop and bought a number of pieces of cooked chicken.

When Farquhar came in she had scraped off the outer orange covering from the chicken pieces and was making a cream-and-cheese sauce. He sniffed, asking what the smell was. She should have buried the chip-shop paper; burning was not possible since they had no fires. But he did not stay to pursue it since he had to change and shave.

'We're off to Louisiana in the morning,' she sang. She feared she had put in a little too much tarragon but a bit of extra seasoning was probably a good idea to suppress the odour of the chip shop.

Farquhar came back, bleeding in the middle of his chin, and with a piece of lavatory paper stuck to the wound.

'You have put the wine in the fridge, haven't you? I asked you to this morning.'

What wine? she was about to ask, but did not need to. He went to the cupboard beneath the stairs and began to rummage about,

48

pulling out old tennis rackets and Wellingtons and hockey sticks. He called for her, demanding to know if she had seen the wine, two bottles of Moselle, or was it possible that the daily help could have helped herself? Emily denied all knowledge. As she said the following day to Louisa, it was the only thing she could have done, otherwise she might have been responsible for giving him a heart attack. Louisa said absolute honesty was not feasible between husband and wife; the relationship was difficult enough without having that as an extra strain imposed upon it.

'Are you certain you put it there, Farquhar?'

'I'm almost sure I did.' He frowned, ruffled up the back of his hair. The lavatory paper had fallen off his chin and blood was oozing down on to his collar.

She suggested that the only way out of the problem was to go and buy two more bottles. There were stores open after six, even if they were not the ones that he preferred to frequent. Muttering to himself, he departed in pursuit of wine and she went back to her sauce which had burnt slightly. She dropped in another handful of cheese, put on the rice and dumped a pound of frozen green beans into a pot.

The Jamieson-Browns arrived two minutes before time, just three minutes after Farquhar had returned and stuck the two bottles he had purchased into the deep freeze. They would never be cold enough otherwise. Douglas Jamieson-Brown was a colleague and lifelong friend; he and Farquhar had been at school and university together, and the two couples had been on visiting terms for all of their married lives. Margo Jamieson-Brown grazed cheeks with her hostess, saying, 'You've cut your hair!' Emily looked at Farquhar but he had not noticed; he was telling Jamieson-Brown about the price his property had fetched at Ravelston that day at noon. Nine thousand over the upset! The men settled into chairs beside one another. Margo asked if there was anything she could do, adding that she was sure Emily would have everything under control, as she always did.

Elspeth and Davina, Farquhar's unmarried elder sisters, arrived together. They did everything together. Twin-setted and strung about with pearls in the daytime, they emerged in the evening in long tartan skirts and white blouses, with steel-grey hair sculpted close to their skulls in finger waves. Relics of a forgotten era, said Camilla, who rummaged in second-hand shops looking for clothes that they might have worn in their younger days. If she followed that track far enough she might end up wearing twin sets and pearls herself, her mother had once said, a remark which had not been well received. Carl had said on one occasion when Emily went to visit at Stockbridge that the aunts – he had been introduced to them in the street – were the bourgeoisie at its most sterile. They were stupid and parasitical, had never earned one penny they lived on. Emily had defended Farquhar's sisters, fairly mildly, saying that they had been born into upper-middle-class Edinburgh life in the Edwardian era, their money had not run out or collapsed through bad investment, and there had been no reason for them to do anything other than they had done. Carl had come back. He enjoyed an argument, especially about the bourgeoisie. Awareness: that was what the aunts were lacking, for if they had had any they would not have been content simply to continue the pattern set up for them, to live in their high Georgian rooms and pretend that the world had not changed all that much. To keep up such a pretence was just possible, if you refused to shop in all those ugly chain stores and scruffy Pakistani grocers, read selected parts of the *Scotsman* and listened only to the third programme on radio. Maybe Elspeth and Davina had chosen, countered Emily; to elect to continue a pattern was as valid a choice as to break it, and, besides, patterns were not so easily broken as talked about, though maybe he and Camilla did not believe that. And perhaps the aunts were unaware, but was that a crime? For Carl it must be, or else one abandoned all responsibility. I didn't know what was happening, I didn't realise . . . That way thousands can be persecuted – *are* persecuted – or put to death, and the remaining millions teeming in the streets and on football terraces, sleeping in front of the telly, hypnotised by Bingo, booze, all the fun of the supermarket, can be looking the other way. Dead easy to look the other way. Dead: that's easy to be too. You just have to walk up the Fall's Road or Sandy Row kicking with the wrong foot, or walk up a white street with a black face, or a black street with a white face, or sit down in a pub for a quiet drink and have a bomb explode under you. The choice is so good nowadays, all the ways you can be a target, in all innocence . . .

You are right, Carl, thought Emily, whilst giving her hot hand into the aunts' cool dry ones, feeling their chins brush her cheek. They smelled of toothpaste and lavender water.

They settled on the settee with glasses of sweet sherry. The women talked of the weather and the prevalence of influenza, and the men continued to exchange notes on the property market, Jamieson-Brown mocking themselves a little for talking shop and saying he hoped the ladies did not mind. Why should they? asked Davina. What a simple soul she is, thought Emily, as she hastened back to the kitchen.

By the time she got it all together, as she put it to herself, everyone was obviously starving. The glasses had long since stood empty; refills, after two, had been declined. They went in to dinner.

They started with tinned tomato soup which she had inadvertently allowed to boil although the directions on the tin strictly forbade it. A dash of cream and a few scatterings of wilted parsley rescued from the refuse bucket had not done much to enhance it. After that came the chicken in cream sauce. It did not look too bad and the dish was admired when she set it on the table. Little was said as eating commenced. Gradually, jaws moved more slowly. The aunts, whose appetites were not robust, gave up halfway, with coughs of embarrassment, putting their knives and forks neatly together, but Margo, who was a woman of great good nature, struggled on until her plate was cleared. The first bottle of wine was nicely chilled and although not brilliant passed muster well enough, as Mountjoy told himself, pouring the end of it into his own glass. When he went to the freezer for the second bottle he found the wine frozen solid. The deep freeze had been set at high. He did his best with the wine under the hot tap but the result verged on the undrinkable. And Jamieson-Brown prided himself on his wines and his knowledge of them! He put his hand over his glass after the first serving. 'No more, thanks, Farquhar, old man. I've got a heavy day tomorrow.'

'Are you going to have a high noon, Douglas?'

'High noon?'

'Just a little joke of Emily's,' said Farquhar hurriedly.

'The chicken was delicious, Emily!' cried Margo.

Emily went to the kitchen and wondered what to bring in for pudding. The choice seemed to be between a block of Neopolitan ice cream which had been in the freezer for a long time and looked it, and tinned pears.

'Rather an undistinguished dessert, I'm afraid,' she said, bringing in both.

'I always run out of steam when it comes to desserts,' said Margo.

The choice of cheese was no better. She carried in a lump of glazed orange Scottish cheddar and a sliver of Jarlsberg, with the same apology.

The coffee was all right. Margo praised it lavishly, asking the name of the blend and where it was purchased, and then led a discussion on coffee prices.

'They say coffee is a drug too, of course, don't they?' said Emily. 'I suppose taken in sufficient quantity it might be as harmful as opium.'

'I hope not,' laughed Margo.

In the middle of coffee Camilla rang. Emily spoke to her in the study. Camilla was indignant; she had ridden all the way out to that God-forsaken wilderness this afternoon on her bicycle and her mother hadn't even been in.

'You can't expect me always to be in.'

'No, but you might have thought I'd come today. After last night.'

Her mother promised to come and see her the following afternoon; she could not stop now for they were in the middle of a dinner party.

'I can imagine!'

'No, Camilla, I doubt if you can.'

The guests left early. After waving them off from the front doorstep, Mountjoy turned to his wife.

'Now, Farquhar, don't start! Anyone can have an off day, cooking-wise, and I do beg your pardon. At least it was only amongst friends.'

'But you don't even seem to be bothered.'

He said not another word to her whilst he undressed, laid his cuff-links on the dressing table, undid his shoe laces, tied the cord of his pyjamas. Every action was laced with hostility. She slid between the sheets and closed her eyes.

At midnight the telephone rang. Farquhar pounced on it, cursing Camilla. But the caller was not their daughter this time; it was someone for Mrs Mountjoy. Emily said she would take it in the study.

Louisa had gone again to see *Long Day's Journey* and was in a mood to talk. She had a theory – O.K., simplistic, she knew – that Conal chose to play fathers because he had never had one himself. Well, there he was as James Tyrone, and next week he'd be Willy Loman, wouldn't he? Emily thought he might have worked through it better by playing sons' parts. 'We usually do things backside-foremost,' said Louisa. She was standing up in the draughty hall at her guest house holding the grey receiver of the wall pay telephone in her hand. Every few minutes she had to feed the slot with money and quieten its bleating. It was bloody barbaric living under such conditions, she said. Emily sat in comfort in Farquhar's deep-buttoned leather chair and thought what a pity it was that Louisa could not have one of their many spare rooms, but that would be stretching Farquhar's tolerance just too far.

At breakfast, he said, 'That woman – that American –' She waited. He was at a loss, did not want to interfere with her friendships, he never had, had he, but did Emily think this woman was suitable for her to have as a friend? What did she *know* about her?

'You can't ask for references, dear. Not like cleaning women. And even they rather resent it nowadays.'

He went to work and she, after her statutory morning chat with her cleaning woman about the state of her varicose veins, husband and neighbours, went to pick up Louisa. They were going to visit a fortified building.

Chapter Four

THE sea lashed the rocks a hundred feet beneath them; bubbling and boiling, it threw spray shooting upward like white fountains. The noise was tremendous. Louisa laughed into the teeth of the gale, her hair whipping straight back from her head revealing the narrowness of its bone structure. One could see how her skull would be, thought Emily, as she clutched her beaver coat about her defying the wind to rip it away and carry it out to the wild waves. A good day to come to Tantallon, Louisa had said earlier as they trudged across the muddy field to reach this impressive and impregnable fortress of the Douglases; it was a wild castle, sternly grand, perched high above the sea, and demanded wild weather.

They were the only visitors.

'Marvellous,' cried Louisa, who would have stayed all day if Emily had not after an hour or so turned blue and begun to tremble. Emily, whilst sheltering in the lee of a wall – the castle was of course roofless – watched Louisa standing on the ramparts gazing out across the Firth and remembered coming here when the children were small and worrying the whole time that they might fall over the cliff and be dashed to pieces on the rocks. She had imagined it happening before her eyes in every detail and had felt sick in the pit of her stomach until they returned to the safety of the car. Many times since then she and Farquhar had driven past and talked of stopping, but never had. Even now she worried about Louisa going too close; the reaction came out of habit, and she was glad when Louisa retreated and joined her on firmer ground. 'But I like going too close to the edge,' said Louisa. 'I want impregnability and proximity to danger at the same time. The one heightens the other.'

Wet and wind-blown, they retreated to a warm hotel to eat and

54

drink. Louisa's eyes glittered. She had taken a number of photographs and planned to return on a sunny day to capture it in a different mood.

'But I think I shall have preferred it in the mood of today. No one would storm such a place on such a day! Not even General Monk.'

Emily raised her glass and drank to that. Her skin was glowing and her lungs felt purged of city air. Not that the air on the Braid Hills was as contaminated as that in the centre of the city, in the Grassmarket, for example, where it was compounded of the odours of exhaust fumes, breweries, and people. Clean air was one reason that Farquhar had been keen to purchase property in their district, the other being that it was a good area which was unlikely to go down. She had not been consulted, except as a mere formality, when she was asked to approve his choice. He would have been astounded if she had not. She remembered that now as she listened to Louisa talk about the kind of house *she* would like to live in. She, Emily Mountjoy, had never given too much thought to the subject. She had always been a very accepting person, she supposed; except once. And then she had rebelled, tried to push back in the face of fate; and had ended exhausted, and at the point where she had begun.

Louisa's exhilaration relaxed her. The hour of respite from making any kind of effort gave her the strength to drive back to Edinburgh and face a visit to her daughter.

Camilla's flat gave no impression of being fortified, or impregnable. The building had suffered from settlement at least once in its hundred or more years of life: the floors sloped, the doors no longer fitted their frames, and a sizeable crack zigzagged down the wall from the ceiling to the skirting board. Two panes of glass in the kitchen window were cracked; one was patched with brown sticky tape, the other shivered restlessly in the wind producing sucking and whistling noises. Anyone might storm this habitation: it would not require a General Monk to punch in the windows, break down the doors, smash up the flimsy furniture, set fire to the heaps of old rags.

Camilla was washing several pairs of pink silk camiknickers in the kitchen sink when she arrived. They were for the shop.

'I'd have thought you'd have left them dirty. Doesn't that add to their desirability?'

Camilla turned to look at her. 'You been taking too many of those pills?'

'Just been drinking.'

Camilla stood with a mass of pink material between her hands dripping water on to her bare feet and stared at her mother. Silk was terribly unabsorbent, observed Emily.

'Mother –'

'Don't worry about me, please, dear. Do get on with your washing. Perhaps I could make us a cup of coffee?'

She made up two mugs of hot liquid with some bottled essence that she associated with the war, whilst Camilla rinsed out the knickers and strung them up on the pulley. Water plopped on to the rush matting at regular intervals. Emily drew her chair to one side. Camilla noticed that she had cut her hair and said thank God she had ceased to look like a cottage loaf at last. Camilla's own hair, which once had shone like ripe corn, now resembled hay which had been subjected to continual soaking and flattening. But that was Camilla's business. She was wearing a kind of Japanese kimono thing, quilted, edged with satin, which someone had probably worn to sit up in bed in at some time, and beneath it she wore a dress of plum-coloured crêpe with a drooping hem and a V-neck, to the point of which clung a diamante clip.

Emily asked after the state of the business and was told they were keeping body and soul together, not much more. But then they didn't want to do any more, they didn't want to become rich off other people's backs. Emily reached for her bag. That reminded her. She had brought some bread and cheese and fruit for them. She didn't have to, said Camilla, to which her mother made the obvious reply, and in the end the gift was accepted and piled on to the table beside various other odds and ends. The room was jammed with objects: fans and feathers, red painted furniture, old tarnished brass bells from tenement flats, Coronation mugs (George VI) battered tea tins, toffee tins, *thé dansant* purses, brass door handles, china waiting to be stuck

56

together, and, of course, clothes. The room smelled overpoweringly of the clothes.

'It's difficult getting stuff these days. Everybody's after it. Don't suppose any of your friends would have anything, would they? What about the old Jimmy-Browns or Mrs Seton?'

Emily said she would ask them but doubted if they would have hung on to their old bread bins and rolling pins. They would probably have consigned them to the dustbin when they bought more up-to-date equipment. No foresight, sighed Camilla. And the aunts Davina and Elspeth were holding on grimly to everything they had. She had had a go at them, wasn't trying to cadge, was prepared to pay, but they had declined politely but firmly. 'We never sell,' they had said.

The door blew open and Carl came in. He directed a nod at Emily, said he was in a hell of a hurry and could he have the camiknickers as he had a bird in the shop who was desperate for them? How could anyone be desperate for such garments? Emily wondered, with genuine interest. She felt that her wonder had reawakened suddenly like a plant that has been long dormant and revived with the necessary food.

'They're still wet, Carl.'

He could not dispute that since a drip had just struck him on the cheek and made him jump. He stared up at the droopy-looking pink silk.

'You should have bloody well washed them earlier instead of lying in your pit stinking! You're a lazy fucking bitch.'

Emily half rose from her hard red chair, sank back. All her instincts aroused in her intense indignation and resentment, and yet she knew he probably spoke the truth. On many occasions she had told Camilla herself that she was lazy, though with less acrimony.

'Fuck off!' screamed Camilla.

He did. The door shuddered for a few seconds before resettling.

'I'm sorry about that,' muttered Camilla.

'That's quite all right, dear. Although I do think he shouldn't speak to you like that. You don't have to put up with it, you know. You could always – ' She broke off. No, Camilla could not always come home. That was unthinkable. 'You could always leave him.'

'I don't want to. We relate to one another, you see. *Do* you see? Did you ever relate to Father?'

'Well –' She considered for a moment, struggling to find the truth. 'In a certain way, I suppose.'

'Oh, not just having it off with him, which I presume you must have done or I wouldn't be here, but really feeling you're in the same groove?'

'But we were in the same groove for a long time.'

'Forget it. Want another coffee?'

Her mother said she must go, she was going to the theatre in the evening. Camilla did not ask to see what, or with whom.

Farquhar did.

'Why should you mind? We've nothing arranged, your dinner's ready. You surely don't mind if I leave you alone for an evening?'

He could not admit to that, which of course she knew, and therefore he was bound to be flummoxed. And no part of her felt that she should relent and change her plans.

Conal's performance engaged her as much as it had the first time, and this she told him when they sat afterwards in the lounge of the Caledonian Hotel drinking brandy. They had decided that it was not worth the effort to frequent pubs late Friday night: conversation was more important than atmosphere. And God help them if they were ever to think otherwise, said Louisa.

Conal was glad they had come this evening, for the following night, the last night of their run, they were due to have an after-the-show party at which he was duty-bound to appear. Duty? asked Louisa. She had imagined it was a concept that would not interest him, unless in relation to his mother. Duty was not the bond there, he said, silencing Louisa, momentarily.

Next week he would be rehearsing *Death of a Salesman* and the week after appear in it, also at the Church Hill, with the Seventies Company, and he hoped they would come to see him in that. He did not need to ask and he knew it. And the week after that production he would be rehearsing *The Plough and the Stars*, which again would be produced the following week.

'And so it goes on?' said Louisa.

'I'm kept busy.'

'Playing only what you want to play?'

58

'Precisely. Is that so dreadful, Louisa?'

'It's wonderful,' cried Emily.

They ended up at Louisa's bed-sit, Mrs McCreedy and Mr Mountjoy being barriers to the other alternatives. Louisa had a bottle of Southern Comfort in her yellow wardrobe.

'Southern Comfort,' said Conal. 'I've always wanted to do some Tennesse Williams. I'll get round to it yet.'

'He doesn't offer much comfort,' said Louisa. 'Or good male parts either. At least, shall we say the female ones steal the lime-light?'

Conal made no reply but poured the liquor into the blue-tinted tumblers which were all that the room could offer. She had more glasses than she could ever use, said Emily, she must give some to Louisa. She had more of most things than she could ever use, in spite of having being burgled; was glutted, longed to strip herself bare, throw out her Edinburgh crystal, damask tablecloths, fine bone tea services, embroidered tray clothes. She confided her desire to them, seated in the pink wicker, gilt-edged chair. It might not necessarily do her any good, said Conal; objects one had gathered were beneficial to most people. But not to Louisa. She travelled light. 'I discard mementos from the past. What good would it do me to be reminded of past failures and suffering?' Conal collected only things that soothed and pleased him. 'You live your life that way though, don't you?' said Louisa. Was there anything wrong with that? he wanted to know. Nothing, cried Emily; it showed only his instinctive wisdom. Louisa did not comment. She reached for the Southern Comfort, refilled their glasses.

Emily sat back, allowing her muscles to slacken. It was such a long time since she had spent evenings this way, talking with people with whom one felt one must inevitably remain friends for life.

Louisa got up and put some music on her hi-fi, one of the few things which she owned in the room. New Orleans Jazz erupted into the room. She invited Conal to dance. He moved sinuously, like someone with a natural rhythm in his body; her movements were more angular, controlled from the head. Emily nodded and swayed in time to the music, from the waist up. She felt possessed

59

of immense perception and of a new energy. It was as if a current in her head had been turned off at some point in the past – turned off but not cut off – and was now switched back on again. She knew, too, at exactly which point the current had been turned off. It was a moment she had worked staunchly to forget over the years. They all had to close wounds, form scabs; or else bleed to death. She thought about that moment now, briefly, and wondered if she might be strong enough to lift the scab, look beneath. And perhaps find that the skin had re-formed and was as good as new? No, she would not expect that.

Louisa was changing the record and Conal was holding out his hand to her. She began to dance. Her body flowed with the music. She became a part of it, and it of her; and the room, and Louisa, were lost to her. Only Conal, moving round her, responding to the same beat, stayed with her. When she held out her hands she could feel the force of his energy flowing into them.

They did not hear the repeated rappings on the door until the record ended. Emily sat down, gasping, rubbing the area over her thudding heart with her right hand. Louisa slid back the snib.

'Miss Grant, I have told you repeatedly – '

Conal, with smoothness, intercepted the landlady's flow. He apologised, expressed dismay, concern. Could it be so late? They had no idea or else they certainly would not have considered disturbing the peace. But the landlady, of many years' experience, was not to be swayed by sweet words and eloquent delivery; she kept a decent house, liked her paying guests to be respectful and respectable, apart from clean and quiet and not leaving a ring round the bath or making a noise in the hall telephoning after eleven o'clock when all good Christian folk should be abed and not bringing in non-residents after midnight. She had been tolerant, had given warning, on more than one occasion, and if folk were going to be so arrogant, so selfish, then she had only one choice left. She must ask Miss Grant to go.

'At this hour?' asked Louisa.

'If you can play yon music at this hour then I can ask you to leave at this hour. But I suppose I'd better let you stay till morning.'

Mrs Mountjoy, rising majestically from the pink and gold wicker chair, informed the landlady that Miss Grant would not dream of staying another five minutes in such a discourteous, inhospitable house, and she would make sure that her husband, a well-known and influential lawyer, would see to it that this was reported to the proper authorities and the house removed from the recommended list for visitors to the Edinburgh Festival.

'Now wait a minute – '

Politely but firmly, Emily eased the woman out and closed the door.

'You were fantastic, Emmie,' said Louisa.

'Pack your bags, Louisa.'

'But where am I to go?'

'Now listen, Emily – '

'Farquhar, what else could I do? Leave her standing in the street? On the main A7, with suitcases, prey for any passing villain to pick her up?'

'She is no little innocent, I'm damned sure of that. I bet she knows exactly what she's about.'

'You don't even know her.'

'That is exactly my objection. I do not want strangers in my house.'

'But she'll not be that for long.'

'Emily, you will remove her from my house as soon as possible.'

He turned as he became aware that someone else had entered the room. Louisa. On soft-heeled feet. He had been so incensed that he had not noticed the door had stood ajar. He was normally a man who made sure that doors were firmly closed before he spoke. It was part of his training.

'I'm so terribly sorry, Mr Mountjoy. I couldn't help hearing...' Louisa said she would leave at once. It had all been just dreadful and the last thing she wanted to do was to cause trouble between him and Emily who had been so incredibly kind to her and of whom she had grown very fond. 'I mean that truly, Mr Mountjoy. Your wife is a wonderful woman.'

Farquhar Mountjoy stood in front of the central-heating radiator, hands behind him, legs astride, in the stance he used to adopt in the days when they had open coal fires. He did not know what to say next since his natural inclination forbade him being rude to a woman, unless it was his own daughter. To Camilla he had been driven into rudeness, inflamed by her own.

'I'll pack my bags, Emily.'

'Farquhar?'

She could stay for a few days, he said, without looking at either of them, whilst she looked for alternative accommodation, and she must realise that he did not wish to be uncivil but he liked to have his house to himself. Oh, she did understand, she said quickly, and it was only natural. She would start to look for an apartment that very day. She rang a few numbers in the *Scotsman* but in all cases was too late, and again when the *Evening News* appeared. Obviously, one had to be sharp off the mark. Perhaps Monday might bring better luck.

Monday brought nothing but a room on the Dalry Road smelling of damp with a leaking roan outside. It was a room in which one might commit suicide, said Emily, refusing to allow her friend to engage it. They had no idea how lucky they were, she told Farquhar, when he was undressing that evening; many people lived in conditions that could only be described as subhuman. That was their fault then on the whole, wasn't it? he said, as he unhooked his braces. At least in the case of Miss Grant it must be. He wasn't prepared to feel sorry for her with two university degrees and four husbands behind her. If she was talking about their cleaning woman who had had to leave school at fourteen and work in a laundry and whose husband drank then he might be prepared to.

He had a way of morally cutting the feet from under her, thought Emily, as she lay between the sheets, waiting for the bed to go down on his side. She did not believe he cared one iota about the cleaning woman. He fell asleep before she did, as usual, and that night his snoring seemed extra loud and persistent and, after an hour or two, became unbearable. The room, her head, reverberated with the noise. They had shared a bed since the day of their marriage. That first night they had met happily enough, he a little clumsy, hesitant, she surprising him with the strength and sureness of her response. If he had realised that she was not a virgin then he had not in any way let her know, and certainly had not questioned her. Sex had never been spoken of between them in a personal sense during all the years they had been together; and now, within the same bed, they slept apart, careful not to let their bodies touch. When they did each drew back as if charged by an electric shock. For some time she had wished that they might have separate beds, and perhaps he had too, but neither had liked to mention it.

She got up, pulled on her dressing gown and went downstairs. She made a pot of tea and carried it into the study. For an hour she read *Death of a Salesman*, which Conal had lent her, and then took herself up to Camilla's room, lifted the teddy bear from the narrow bed and crept inside. Immediately, she fell into a peaceful sleep, wakening to see sunlight on a print of pre-Raphaelite women and hear Farquhar's voice calling below. She picked up the teddy bear and fingered it, touching the button eyes, the torn ear, the worn fur, remembering the day Camilla received it. She had so much wanted to be a wife and mother, had had so little idea of what it would really be like. It was the estrangement from them that had taken her so much by surprise. They came back later, people said, but the boy was gone so far and now had married a girl out there. When he left she had tried not to dwell too much on his going, to let herself become morbid or maudlin – his loss *was* exceedingly painful to her – but since meeting Conal she had found that she had been able to think about her son with less pain. Something about Conal reminded her of James. His *joie de vivre* perhaps. From the moment James opened his eyes he had appeared to find the world to his liking.

Her husband was still calling, his voice rising, as if he feared another kidnapping. With a rush of compassion, she rose and went to him, but was unable to get a word out before he did.

'Now I know you're going through a difficult time of life, Emily, but I refuse to be made to look like a fool.'

'No one is looking at you, Farquhar.'

'*She* is in the house.'

'She doesn't know where I slept. Or that you thought I was lost again.'

'I've a feeling she knows everything.'

'How irrational of you, Farquhar!'

'There's something menacing about her, I don't know what it is. But I don't trust her.'

He did not trust anyone he did not know or who did not come from his own millieu, she claimed. That was untrue, he retaliated, he could cite a dozen cases to disprove it, but the whole tone of the conversation was ridiculous and he wished to terminate it at once. He terminated everything that was not going his way, she maintained, but he was not going to listen, was already striding off to the peace of his study, where he might shut the door and call his soul his own. But even there all was not of his arranging for the first thing that attracted his eye was an opened copy of *Death of a Salesman* lying on his desk. He looked back at the fly-leaf. Conal McCreedy. Who on earth was he? He disliked the look of the name, mistrusted it. No doubt he was a friend of Louisa's. He mistrusted Louisa: that was not in any doubt. Since Emily had met up with her she had been acting very strangely and it had even crossed his mind that she might be taking drugs, ones other than those prescribed by the doctor. That American woman might have given them to her and in the mood she was in Emily was damned fool enough to try anything. When they went out he would search Louisa's luggage. You couldn't be too careful about such matters. What would it look like if *he* was found to be harbouring a drug pusher? He shook his head sharply. He was letting his imagination run riot, doing an Emily! But, nevertheless, it would do no harm if he did have a look at the woman's stuff. He slammed the book shut and tossed it on to a chair.

It was a Sunday morning and he forgot to go to church.

Louisa was getting ready to go to Mass at the University Chaplaincy centre.

'Were you born and bred a Catholic?' asked Emily.

'No, I got converted last year.' Before that, Louisa had been a number of things: Methodist, Christian Scientist, Zen Buddhist. 'Etcetera. One must experiment, don't you think? At least you know in the end what you've chosen amongst.'

'Do you know, I've never been to a Catholic service? Except for standing at the back at Nôtre Dame.'

'Come with me then!'

Kneeling beside them in the pew were Conal and his mother.

After the service they promenaded around George Square together, Conal and Louisa walking in front talking about Sir Walter Scott who had once been an inhabitant, and Emily coming behind, more slowly, with Mrs McCreedy. The little dressmaker looked even smaller out of her room and she walked jerkily as if she was not used to stretching her legs over such a distance. Mrs Mountjoy said how nice it would be when spring came and the trees had some green on them again and the daffodils bloomed in the gardens. She recalled how as a student she had delivered Christmas mail here and all the square had been complete in its Georgian splendour and now, sadly, only one side remained intact, and the university towers loomed above displaying their crassness and ignorance. Within Conal's proximity, she found she waxed much more eloquently. Strange that it should be so, that even articulacy should be catching.

'Much is catching in life, don't you think so, Mrs McCreedy?'

The dressmaker could not agree. She caught little from the women who came and went in her room exposing their backs and bosoms and talking of their private lives. Many treated her like a priest in the confessional; stripped of clothing, they unburdened their souls also, confessing to crimes both sexual and spiritual. She had always told them that they were overestimating the importance of their sins when it came to the flesh. A mere coupling with another body did not matter. The Good Lord would take no notice of that, no more than she did when Conal had a lady in his room. On such occasions she did what she could to take no notice either; she'd put her foot on the pedal of her treadle sewing machine and pedal furiously, letting the material fly between her fingers, and the noise would drown out any sounds that might come through from the back of the flat. She knew that Conal needed the release of the flesh, would not attempt to deny him that. All the time she walked beside Mrs Mountjoy, who was expounding on her theme of infectiousness, she kept her eyes on the back of the American girl. She did not believe that Louisa was his type at all; he liked voluptuous women, well endowed in the breast and hip; but she could see that *he* might be Louisa's type. Most women liked Conal. It was unusual when one did not.

'Did you go to see Conal in his play?' asked Mrs Mountjoy.

Mrs McCreedy had not, and never did go to see him; she did not care for going out in the evenings and even her daytime outings were limited to the half-mile stretch between the Grassmarket and George Square. Home and church were all that she required. Mrs Mountjoy was astonished, thought she would have wanted to see Conal perform. But she did, she said, in front of her own hearth; he went through the entire play for her and she heard his lines and so by the time the first night arrived she knew it as well as he. She had no interest in seeing any of the others.

'What a self-contained woman she is,' said Emily after they had taken leave of the McCreedys.

'She still contains Conal in her womb. Oh yes! Her room is merely an extension of it, she was not prepared to push him out any further.'

Over lunch, Louisa said, 'I took your wife to Mass this morning, Mr Mountjoy.'

It was a most unfortunate statement to have made, and afterwards Louisa apologised to Emily for it.

Chapter Five

SITTING in Mrs McCreedy's room – or womb, as she now inevitably thought of it, although the concept did seem a trifle bizarre, even obscene – Emily watched Louisa having a fitting. The dressmaker, with a battery of pins in her mouth, moved slowly round her client's body, her eyes peering from behind their thick shields, a frown puckering her forehead, both hands working, easing, tweaking, smoothing, pinning. Her concentration was so total that it precluded conversation. Louisa swayed a little as if mesmerised and, indeed, said later that she had felt held in the little woman's power, which, on being released from it, made her behave in a slightly heady way.

When the dress was pinned and held, Mrs McCreedy squatted back on her haunches to regard it for a moment, then she nodded. She stood up and helped to ease the material over Louisa's head, taking care that no pin should scrape her skin. As she lifted it clear, Louisa's arm jerked out and her fingertips caught the edge of the dressmaker's spectacles throwing them in a wide arc across the room. To the onlookers' startled eyes, they seemed to move in slow motion, making the moment before they struck the floor appear endless. It was as if the world had slowed down. Mrs McCreedy stood still, transfixed like a child frozen in a game of statues. The other two women stared at her naked eyes with a sense of shock which they saw reflected in them. The material slid to the ground, and the dressmaker held out both hands, palms upward, fingers curling inward. She looked like a beggar seeking alms.

'Gee, Mrs McCreedy, what an idiot I am!' Louisa was half giggling. 'Now stay where you are, don't move! I'll get them for you.' She swooped down on the spectacles, scooped them up and held them aloft. 'Got them! No harm done.'

67

'Give them to me.' The hands inched forward.

'Let me put them on for you.'

'No. Put them in my hands, *please*.'

'Oh, come now, Mrs McCreedy, you just stand still and I'll put them on for you.'

Emily watched Louisa take off her own glasses and place the legs around the dressmaker's ears. Then she took the thick ones and put them on herself. She staggered like a drunk, lurching crazily from side to side.

'What have you done?' cried Mrs McCreedy, putting her hands to the sides of her head.

'We've swopped glasses! Gosh, now I can't see a thing. The room's swimming, it's like being in an aquarium. I can see red and purple and green all blurred running together. Where are you, Emily?'

Louisa stood in the middle of the room clothed only in her underwear and the little round pebbled glasses, and laughed. She went on laughing. And Emily stared, unable to move or speak.

'Give me my glasses back!' cried Mrs McCreedy.

'O.K., O.K! I'm just going to.' Swiftly now Louisa changed the spectacles. 'There you are! It was just a joke, Mrs McCreedy. You didn't mind, did you? Come on, you're not cross with me, are you?'

The dressmaker did not answer. She lifted the material from the floor and straightened it out. Louisa looked at Emily, shrugged, and went to the window. The sun was shining, the day was unexpectedly mild, offering promise that spring would come eventually, even if it would not be this month or next.

'What a gorgeous day!' Louisa stretched out her arms. 'Can I open the window for a second, Mrs McCreedy?'

At once she flung it up and leaned out across the sill. The two women left within the room gazed at the small thin bottom covered with a strip of cotton. The rest of her was not visible.

'Mind you don't fall, Louisa!' cried Emily, remembering how Camilla used to hang from upstairs windows to frighten her.

Louisa pulled her head back in and laughed. She closed the window, dusted off her hands on the sides of her thighs.

'You mustn't mind me, Mrs McCreedy. I'm kind of impetuous

at times. Don't you think people can be too inhibited? I'm all for unblocking behaviour. Do you know, when I was looking down I could just imagine what it would have been like in the seventeenth century. I could see the throngs of people and carts and horses. The moment I arrived in Edinburgh I felt I belonged. I had an incredibly strong feeling of *déja vû*, as if I must have been here at some other time. And perhaps I was. In the seventeenth century!' She was in no hurry to replace her clothes; she wandered over to the far wall to look again at a picture of Conal. 'Did you get a sense of instant belonging when you first arrived, Mrs McCreedy?'

'I can't say I did.'

'It grew on you?'

Mrs McCreedy shrugged.

She is only aware of her room, thought Emily.

The doorbell rang. Mrs McCreedy excused herself and went to answer it, clicking the door shut behind her.

'I've shocked you, haven't I, Emily?'

'No, no.'

'I have, I can see I have. I didn't mean any harm. Sometimes a kind of little devil gets inside me. Just a very little one though.' Louisa broke off to listen.

A voice was raised in the passage. 'I want to see him. I'm going to see him!'

'He's not at home, I tell you. And now would you please go? I have a customer.'

'You always have a customer. He's probably in there with her.'

The door opened and a woman of middle age burst in, stumbling over a dummy dressed in turquoise satin and setting it rocking. She glared at them. Behind her, Mrs McCreedy was invisible, but could be heard. She was demanding that she leave at once. Without a word the woman turned, breathing heavily, and went through the narrow passage into Conal's room. A few seconds later they heard her leave, slamming the front door.

'Terrible what drink does to folk,' said Mrs McCreedy. 'She was a decent enough woman once but now – '

They waited but she was not prepared to divulge anything more. They must leave now: she was busy, wanted her room cleared of intruders. She was a woman full of secrets, said Louisa, as they descended the stairs; no one, not even her son, would know what went on behind those thick glass walls. They stepped into the street still thinking of the woman who had barged into the flat looking for Conal. Emily supposed the women who were slumped against the wall waiting for the Salvation Army hostel to open were decent enough too once. They passed the one who forever seemed to be urinating. The women seemed more pathetic than the men, did Louisa not think so? That was because women were more highly censored when they lost their dignity, said Louisa; it was still easier to be eccentric and male, than odd and female. On their way up the Grassmarket they saw the rejected women leaning against the window of a clothes boutique smoking a cigarette. She was watching the McCreedys' stair door.

They did not mention the woman to Conal when they rendez-voused that evening. He was rehearsing for *Death of a Salesman* in a church hall in Corstorphine. They drove out to meet him.

When the hall door opened a bunch of people in woollen hats emerged emitting bursts of chat and laughter. Conal detached himself from them and crossed the street.

'They seem excited,' said Louisa, as he ducked into the back of the car.

'There's always a slight bit of hysteria before a show.'

They waved back to the woollen hats.

Louisa had plans for the three of them but before putting them into effect they went for a drink in a quiet corner of a hotel so that Conal could unwind and ease himself out of the character of Willy Loman. Over the first drink he sat slumped, looking middle-aged, his mouth sagging, his forehead creased. He looked like a failed man. Louisa talked about Miller and his social commitment and his search for root causes. 'He comes in at the end but digs back into the past relentlessly searching for the root cause.' Louisa looked at Conal and then at Emily. 'You two never talk about your pasts. You're closed tight like clams. You try to pretend nothing exists beyond yesterday. Whereas I have told you a hell of a lot about my past.' The allegation was not quite fair, thought Emily, for she had told odd snippets, though they of course had nothing to do with root causes. But she did not wish to argue with, or challenge, Louisa, and neither did Conal. They allowed her to continue on her track of self-alienation. Her voice was quite soothing, even hypnotic.

Gradually, Conal unwound; his face became firmer and younger, the pucker left his eyebrows. Louisa came to the end of her dissertation and subsided. Emily called for another round of drinks. It was a hell of a drain being an actor, said Conal, and sometimes on waking one wondered who one really was. Louisa knew the feeling. Well, of course! Hadn't she had four other surnames before reverting back to her original one of Grant? But Emily knew that she was Emily Mountjoy. If someone was to call to her by her maiden name now she would not even turn her head. Emily Dickson? Who was she? A girl who stood on the other side of the river bank.

They proceeded then to Tiffany's. This was going to be a completely new experience for her, said Emily happily, as they eased past a couple of taxis disgorging fellow revellers into St Stephen Street, the narrow street where Camilla and Carl lived. It was unlikely though that they would be inside a nightclub; they sought less synthetic pleasures.

The pleasures were noisy and smoky, whatever else they were. For a moment Emily felt stunned by the bombardment to her senses and hesitated, uncertain in which direction to move, until Conal's hand came under her elbow and he guided her into a seat. It was not quite her scene either, yelled Louisa, but she felt they should explore every avenue open to them, to the extent of at least traversing it once. It wouldn't take long to get through them, not in Edinburgh, said Conal, who was able to project his voice without shouting and straining his throat. On some evenings ladies wrestled here in mud, he said, not that he had seen, or wished to see, them, and then on others there was punk rock. The group came to the end of a number and for a few minutes they could converse in fairly normal tones. The place was packed and to Emily's eyes most of the girls looked about fifteen. She was easily the oldest woman in the room, though a number of men with their arms round the girls might match her in age.

'There are a couple of gaming joints we could also try. "I'm a

rambler, I'm a gambler, I'm a long way from home",' sang Conal,
' "and if moonshine won't kill me I'll live till I die." One of
my da's old songs, so my mother once told me in an unusual fit
of nostalgia.'

'Yes, I would imagine your mother did not often give way to
nostalgia,' said Louisa.

The music started up again and Louisa and Conal got up to
dance. Sipping gin, Emily sat and watched, observing, as she
put it to herself, all the varieties of human behaviour. Such
phrases amused her and made her want to laugh aloud. Laughter
all around her was uproarious, speech loud, passions heated; or
gave the appearance of being so. The couple at the next table
were glued lip to lip, body to body, he almost lying upon her.
She wondered if they were about to have full sexual intercouse
right in front of everybody. And then the man sat up and
yawned and scratched his left ear. He looked bored. Emily smiled
at him. He got up and came to her. He was asking her to dance.
His words were inaudible but his gestures were obvious. Glancing
at the girl from whom he had so recently prised himself loose,
Emily saw that she looked unconcerned, was yawning and frowning into a pocket mirror, now beginning to squeeze a spot on her
chin.

Emily stood up and went forward into the man's arms.

She twisted and rocked or bopped, she did not know what, for
all those modes of dancing she had missed out on, having given
up going to dances other than dinner ones since her pre-Farquhar
days. The samba and the tango were for her the most demanding
that she had ever been asked to execute but even these now she
no longer stood up for, limiting her appearances on the dance
floor to the old-fashioned waltz and the Gay Gordons. By the end
of one number she was gasping for breath and had damp patches
under her arms like half-moons.

'You were great, hen,' said her partner, leading her back to
her table. Conal bought him a drink. His girl had gone, found
someone else. She was a pain in the neck, he said, no great loss,
had nothing to say for herself. He liked a bit of conversation himself. His name was Alec and he was a stonemason to trade, working
at present on a New Town conservation project. He was able to

give Louisa lots of interesting details about Georgian building. Conal took Emily up to dance.

'Fancy me at my age!'

'You look in your element!'

She felt it and the feeling was not diminished even when she saw one or two of the young girls eyeing her with amusement. Let them laugh! They spent the rest of the evening with Alec. He seemed pleased to have their company and asked numerous questions of Louisa about life in Chicago and the United States generaally, which gave Louisa lots of scope. And so they talked and drank and danced and Emily found herself gradually becoming acclimatised until she no longer gasped for breath. It was a relief to know that she was still capable of finding a second wind.

The final dance of the evening she had with Conal, and in the last few spinning seconds when the music seemed to get more and more hectic and the beat within her increased to keep pace with it, she staggered, lost balance, and fell. She lay on the ground only for one second for Conal, attentive and quick in his responses, immediately brought her back to her feet. The drums rolled and crashed to a crescendo. Was she all right? He was solicitous, concerned, bending to look at the ankle which she was rubbing. She was fine, she said, one of her automatic responses, but she had, in fact, staved her ankle. She hobbled back to their table, laughing, mocking herself, making light of her injury. An old lady like her shouldn't take up dancing! Old lady nothing, said Conal. He helped her to the car, and she leant against him enjoying the warmth and strength of his body. It was obvious she would not be able to drive, Conal could not, and Louisa did not have a U.K. driving licence. That left Alec.

'Why not all come back to my place for coffee?'

Farquhar was in bed, though not asleep. He was holding a paperback copy of an Alastair Maclean novel in front of him.

'You've been drinking, Emily! I can smell your breath from here. And you reek of cigarette smoke.' He looked over the edge of the bed. 'What on earth have you done to your ankle?'

Louisa had bathed the foot with hot and cold water and bound it with a bandage. Emily said that she had slipped going down a broken kerb.

'You are making a ridiculous exhibition of yourself, you know.'

She did not bother to deny it but went on to tell him that he should not keep the light on for her as she had brought some friends in for coffee. Oh, no one he knew, some people she and Louisa had met at a lecture. He would not come down, he would fear a ridiculous scene in which he might flounder; she counted on that. He would not come and throw them out as he had done Camilla's friends on previous occasions. She went downstairs to serve her guests coffee and brandy in the drawing room.

Farquhar remained upstairs, trapped within his room, and read occasional, disconnected lines of Alastair Maclean's which naturally did not make any sense. It was unfortunate that their bedroom was directly over the drawing room. From below came the sound of lively conversation that from time to time swelled to what he could only presume was heated argument. Then he laid his book aside. But the arguments always died down again and often ended in gusts of laughter. Doors opened, feet went to and fro, the lavatory cistern emptied and filled.

After one particularly loud burst of laughter he pushed back the covers and slid his feet into his slippers. He pulled on his camel-coloured dressing-gown. Quietly, tiptoeing almost, he went towards the door pausing a moment there to listen. All noise appeared to be confined to the ground floor.

He opened the door and went out on to the landing where he stood with his hands on the rail listening to the sound of their revelry. Yes, they were revelling : no other word would describe it. The noise echoed in the stair well, filled the house. It was as well they were detached; otherwise there would have been neighbours on the doorstep by this time. Underneath him, the drawing-room door opened. He crouched down, letting his hands slide down the wrought-iron railings. Peering between them, he saw the foreshortened figure of a man in a blue suit crossing the hall. He was stocky, wide-shouldered, with a balding patch in the centre of dark hair, and he walked jauntily, splaying out his knees.

'Third door on the right, Alex.' Emily's voice rang out clearly, and for a moment her husband did not recognise it.

'Right you are, Emmie !'

Alex went into the downstairs toilet. Farquhar Mountjoy, his knees trembling foolishly within their camel covering, rose up and returned to his room.

At three o'clock the two men left in a cab, calling out rather loud goodbyes from the gate. Suddenly, Emily felt exhausted. She needed to be alone. Her head was ringing with arguments about nationalism and internationalism, society and the self, good and evil. They had got on to the latter when she had defended Farquhar against charges of male chauvinism (from Alec, surprisingly) by saying that he was a good man. 'He would not willingly do evil.' Was that the definition of a good man? demanded Louisa. 'Is there such a thing as a wholly good or bad man anyway?' said Conal. Emily had withdrawn the epithet she had ascribed to Farquhar, agreeing that they were all mixtures of good and evil; it was the degree of each that was the important thing. 'A matter of degree,' she murmured, as she stood before the bathroom mirror and saw her face reflected there, slack and putty-coloured, blotched with brown spots between the eyelids and the brows. She let the muscles sag accentuating the lines until they verged on the grotesque, then hastily she turned away.

She decided that she would not disturb Farquhar, whom she hoped slept; she would spend the night in Camilla's bed again and cuddle her teddy bear. The bed offered peace, a return to a former state of bliss, when time held no terror and anxieties were but passing whims that slipped away into the shadows when one closed one's eyes. *Whisper who dare . . .*

In the morning Farquhar said nothing. He spooned up his porridge as if it were curds and arsenic. He wiped the top of his small moustache with the edge of his table napkin. He rolled the napkin into a tight roll and imprisoned it in its silver ring. He excused himself. He pushed back his chair and rose.

Louisa was spending the morning at the library, and Emily had been scheduled for a Yoga lesson. The ankle injury, however, ruled that out. She had already had one lesson and found it much less of an ordeal than she had feared. In fact, it had been a pleasure. She had spread her tartan travelling rug on a rather dirty hall floor along with a number of other women of varying ages and sizes (the variation, in itself, had reassured her) and had proceeded to persuade her body to shape itself into some amazing poses which she might have been inclined to dismiss as impossible. To the cheerful, supple teacher nothing was impossible. Only try, she kept saying, don't be afraid to try. To make a fool of oneself was not possible either. And this was what Emily had been most afraid of. Greatly heartened, she had gone at the end of the lesson for coffee with the other women, had listened to tales about their children and sympathised with their struggles to make ends meet. She felt a genuine curiosity about their lives, banal and unexciting though they might be judged, and did not have to feign interest. She was aware that they, too, had their dark times when they knew the stab of anguish that feels like a knife turning in the heart, as well as the brilliant pinpricks of joy that come at the most unexpected moments, even though they spoke only of rising prices and compared notes on the development of their children.

She smiled, thinking of them now spreadeagled on their rugs, and turned her attention to a quite different woman. Louisa had given her the journals of Anaïs Nin to read. She lay on the couch and allowed herself to be bewitched by the elegant silver prose. Such a sensitive quivering woman! Not at all interested in prices and superficial minutiae, but seeking always to go deeper, to try to understand herself and others, not shying away from the truth even when it became painful. How difficult that was! Emily sighed, but softly, not feeling in any way dispirited.

The hours slipped away smoothly. At intervals, the cleaning woman, on some pretext or other looked in and sniffed at the sight of Mrs Mountjoy lazing on the sofa with a book in the middle of the morning. Emily found she was enjoying the lull, the break from mad careering, although by evening she would rally again and be ready to place her bets on the roulette wheel, if necessary. Mrs Seton phoned to say what about lunch and Mrs Mountjoy was pleased to be able to plead indisposition. Camilla phoned to ask had she made any progress with Mrs Seton.

'Oh, you mean about bread tins and flannel nightdresses?'

'Anything.' Camilla sounded irritable.

'I wonder if you don't need some iron pills, love? You always do tend to be a bit anaemic, especially at the back end of the winter.'

'Mother!'

'Sorry, dear.'

She limped back to her sofa.

When the cleaning woman looked in and sniffed the next time she added, 'There's a man here to see you.'

It was Conal.

'Don't get up.' He came to her, took her hand and kissed it, as he had the first night she drove him home.

'Will there be anything else, Mrs Mountjoy?'

'Perhaps you'd bring us some coffee, Mrs Lamb?'

Mrs Lamb had sponged the stain off the front of her overall and rearranged her thin auburn hair before she came back carrying a tray set with an embroidered cloth and the coffee things. On it also was a plate of chocolate biscuits tastefully displayed. She liked things to be tasteful, she always told Mrs Mountjoy. Conal jumped up at once to help her with the tray, and she, protesting, allowed him to put his hands on it and together they laid it to rest on the coffee table. She smiled sideways at him. She'd seen him before, hadn't she, on the telly? It was possible, he admitted. Milk and sugar? she asked, forgetting Mrs Mountjoy who reclined on the settee looking on. 'I know,' she said suddenly. 'You were in an ad for beer! You were drinking a pint of heavy, leaning on the counter talking to another chap who was drinking the wrong brand. I thought you'd ever such a nice voice.' How kind of her, he said, and went on to recall, for her benefit, how long the clip had taken to make, and how he had had to say the same line more than fifty times till they got everything exactly right. Mrs Lamb was impressed, would have something extra to tell the neighbours tonight. By the time she left them – some folks must work – Emily's coffee was cold but she did not mind for she still had Conal.

He stayed for lunch, which they ate in the kitchen, and from behind a bundle of rotting gym shoes in the hall cupboard she unearthed a dusty old bottle of Beaujolais. His arrival merited some sort of celebration. It was noble of him to have come all this way out to the suburbs to inquire after her ankle; she knew how much he disliked leaving the city centre. He drank a toast to her good health, and said that he had come because he wanted to see her and did not mind how many rings of time he had to travel through to do that. He would be prepared even to pierce the sound barrier. She shuddered. That sounded much too painful, apart from not being necessary. The kitchen was peaceful, being at the back of the house; they looked out on the garden and the high pink stone wall that surrounded it. In early summer the gean and lilac trees were beautiful; their blossoms clouded the world with pink and white and often she sat on the bench and let them float before her eyes. She wanted to tell him about everything that pleased her and he seemed to want to hear for he listened and nodded and found nothing odd, not even when she told him how she liked to lie in Camilla's narrow bed.

Camilla arrived when they were at the coffee stage, pushing her bicycle past the kitchen window; she looked up and saw them gazing out at her and halted, hands square on the handlebars. She stared back at them. Her mother waved her in.

She and Conal did not take to one another. Strange, wasn't it? she said to Louisa later, but Louisa did not think so. Young girls did not interest Conal and so he did not put himself out to interest them; he preferred older women. Emily knew this herself but enjoyed hearing Louisa articulate it. Conal and Camilla exchanged a few banal little sentences and then he left.

'What was *he* doing here?'

'Having lunch, dear. What did it look like?'

Camilla muttered something about not trusting him if it were her. She opened the fridge door and raked amongst the shelves. 'He's probably out for what he can get.'

'In what way do you mean, dear.'

'Anything.' Camilla began to munch on a chicken leg, tearing off pieces of flesh with her strong white teeth. When she lived at home she had always been a compulsive fridge raider, had got up in the middle of the night to devour the most incredible quantities of food, so that her mother would never be sure of what she would find in the morning and what she would not.

In many ways her daughter was the most terrible prude but she did not dare to say so for that would have evoked a storm which she had no wish either to combat or take shelter from. They had had storms enough in the past to last more than a lifetime; in retrospect they appeared to Emily as futile exercises, except to provide release from tension. Today, she felt no tension.

When Camilla had finished eating she noticed that her mother's leg was shrouded with a bandage and propped on a chair. At once she was full of concern, offering to shop and cook. But there was no need for Louisa was going to do all that and was making them a New England boiled dinner tonight.

'Louisa?'

'You must stay and meet her.'

'She's the spitting image of her father,' said Louisa afterwards. 'Didn't take to me either, did she? No, don't protest. I can accept that, Emily. She sees me as an intruder, which of course I am. The stranger inside the gate.'

Farquhar ate his boiled dinner. He wiped his moustache with the edge of his napkin. He said that that was very nice. No, he did not wish a dessert, thank you, even though Louisa had made lemon meringue pie which was a favourite of his. He excused himself and rose. From the door he looked back and asked if he might have a word with his wife.

He was treading his study floor. The boards were creaking.

'You must ask her to go, Emily.'

'What harm is she doing, Farquhar?'

'She is – ' He drew in his breath.

'What?'

'She is leading you astray.'

She laughed so much she had to sit down. She laughed until she had to put her hand below her breast.

'I don't want to sound pompous but you are making me, God damn you!'

She knew, and was sorry. She sobered. She wanted to be reasonable and yet unreasonable. Could he not understand? Time was running out. They were not as young as they used to be, it would be a sin to waste one's last years doing all the things one did not want to do. He froze at that. He must go on selling houses until he was sixty-five, write ads for the *Scotsman*, dwelling on desirable flats, superb views; he must keep in with clients and not antagonise other solicitors. Why didn't he retire now? she suggested. They could sell the house, buy a small flat and concentrate all their energies on living.

'Have you gone mad, Emily? I like my work, I enjoy my work, I believe in my work.'

'All right, Farquhar.' Far be it for her to try to shake him from that. But he was launched and his flow would not be staunched until it had flooded out, even though the views had been aired many times before. It was becoming quite the thing now for people not to work, not if they could cadge off the state or somebody else. She wondered how he could go on repeating the same things without boring himself, but then people did repeat themselves all the time. Look at Carl and Camilla! Call that work? Look at Louisa! Call that work? Somebody was financing her so that she could write a thesis on the toilet habits of American women who had flitted through Scotland or some damned fool thing like that. These academics were all the same, pursuing trifles, giving into minor byways that no one but them gave tuppence about. Did Charles Lamb meet Wordsworth in Wigan on a dirty day in February? Who the hell cared? Should care? No wonder the world was in such a state. It would be more peaceful, ventured Emily, if everyone pursued such things.

'But futile. And decadent. We are surrounded by futility and decadence. There is our daughter expensively educated selling old clothes.'

'Recycling them.'

'Pah!'

'But you are recycling houses, Farquhar.'

He sat down at his desk. He put his elbows on the blotter and his head between his hands. He stared down at the *Journals of Anaïs Nin*. He looked at the inside page and read the name 'Louisa Flora Grant'. That bloody woman was infiltrating everywhere. His study, his stomach, his wife. His wife? God, surely not! Ten years ago it would have been unthinkable – he would not have thought it – but now – He looked up at his wife.

'Farquhar, let Louisa stay just a little longer till we see how things go. You see, she's company for me. And I do need a companion.'

'Oh, all right!'

She thanked him and could imagine Camilla's voice saying that it was preposterous that she should have to thank her husband for letting her have a friend to stay in her own home. She dismissed Camilla's voice. Would Farquhar like her to stay in with him that evening? They might have a game of backgammon if he wished. But he had a meeting at the golf club, something rather important had come up and since he was on the committee . . . That was quite all right, she assured him, her heart leaping at the reprieve. Another evening of freedom lay ahead. They were going gambling, she and Conal and Louisa. Another first for her.

She was ten pounds up at the end of the evening. She was a lucky lady, said Conal, in a gypsy voice, taking her hand in his to read the palm and tell her she would live to be a hundred and two and have twenty children. He circled his finger round the middle of her palm, tickling it and making her laugh.

Round and round the garden goes the teddy bear. One step, two steps . . .

Chapter Six

MRS MOUNTJOY went alone for her fitting, preferring it that way, for she still felt modest where her body was concerned, an inhibition she could not shed as easily as some others. In front of Mrs McCreedy she felt no embarrassment; it was a bit like going to the doctor. Without Louisa the room was more peaceful, that was undeniable. Louisa added a charge to the atmosphere; she was like a current of energy giving life, which Emily welcomed much of the time, though on occasions needed a rest from it, a fact which Louisa herself appreciated. She was perceptive and sensitive. She had established a modus vivendi for herself in the Mountjoys' house by tucking herself away in her back room when Farquhar was at home, not even eating with them, but cooking snacks for herself when the kitchen was clear. For days she and Farquhar did not see one another. In the evenings, if they were not going out, Emily would slip up to Louisa's room where they would discuss castles, fortified houses and American women. Emily herself had spent several days in the library in pursuit of the latter but had not had much luck finding Scottish connections, although she had enjoyed herself thoroughly. She had browsed through biographies of Fitzgerald and Henry James and Dreiser, dipped into poems of Whitman, Thoreau and Eliot (even though none were women) and then had turned her attention to Ella Wheeler Wilcox – for a moment she had thought she was on to a winner there on finding a poem entitled *The Brave Highland Laddies* but then discovered that Ella Wheeler Wilcox had seen them parading through Piccadilly – Willa Cather, Carson McCullers, Marianne Moore, Edna St Vincent Millay, Emily Dickinson. The indexes revealed nothing under Scotland, though often there was an entry under Scott which she would flip up. It proved to be a most enjoyable way to spend a day and she became interested especially in the poetry and life of Emily Dickinson. It was the name that drew her, so like her own maiden one. No real progress, though, she was sorry to have to report to Louisa, who remained undismayed; she was confident that something would turn up. That was the joy of research: the hope of finding a clue which would open a gate and lead one onward. She was making progress on her own obsession, making notes, taking photographs, dying for spring to come when many establishments would open their doors to the public. By the time she finished she would have enough material for a lecture tour. Was that what lay behind it then? asked Emily. Not really, said Louisa; but she felt it good always to be prepared, to have things tucked away like pre-cooked meals in a deep freeze ready to be brought out for unexpected company. Emily, face to face with Louisa, felt exceedingly unprepared for life, could give a lecture on nothing, not even motherhood or housewifery, at which she had spent the greater part of her life.

'And how's your American friend?' asked the dressmaker, taking the last pin from her mouth.

'Very well.' Emily went on to make a special plea for Louisa, saying that she was high-spirited at times and Mrs McCreedy must not take offence, for she felt confident that none was meant.

'I'm blind without my glasses, Mrs Mountjoy.'

'I know, and I am sorry about that.'

The dressmaker was sitting back on her heels frowning. Was there anything the matter? Mrs Mountjoy had lost weight since being measured and she was going to have to take the dress in at least an inch all round. Emily's heart rose. Amazing that such a banal piece of good news should give one such a lift! She beamed down on the dressmaker's head as if it were she who had personally bestowed the gift. But she had been eating less recently, indulging in fewer cream buns and slabs of chocolate cake to shorten lengthy afternoons. Now the days were fully taken from the moment of rising to start on Farquhar's porridge, and although her alcohol consumption had risen she presumed that the extra energy she was using up was compensating for that. When she told Conal and Louisa, he said, 'Don't lose too much. I like you as you are,' and Louisa murmured, 'You are all for softness, aren't you, Conal? Maternal bosoms to lay your head upon?' Seeing the look on Emily's face, she added quickly, 'Oh, don't take me seriously, Emmie! I am just jealous!' Conal said she had no need to be; he liked her the way she was too. Each person should be different, the craze for standardisation was appalling, with everyone struggling to reach the same statistics and standards. It was unlikely that Mrs McCreedy had ever tried to reach any kind of ideal, except perhaps in her needlework where her standard was one of near perfection. Conal said that she would unpick and remake and unpick again until she got a piece of work right. Just as he worked at his parts, never satisfied, always self-critical. He was opening tonight in *Death of a Salesman*. Last night he had been tearing himself apart with criticism after the dress rehearsal.

The day was dwindling, the light outside going leaving a smear of dark pink and indigo behind the rooftops. Would Mrs Mountjoy care to take a little refreshment with her? asked Mrs McCreedy. Mrs Mountjoy was her last customer of the day and when she finished work it was her habit to treat herself to a dram or two. Emily was gratified, and accepted at once, settling into the large leather armchair which was Conal's. His mother sat opposite in a lower chair, her feet on the fender, her skirt pulled up so that she might warm her knees. They looked puffy and the flesh swelling upward from them was marked with dark, raised veins, visible even through her stockings.

'You've had to work hard all your life, Mrs McCreedy.'

'I may not be able to work much longer. My eyes are getting worse.'

Emily felt shocked. Mrs McCreedy without her dressmaking? Her room stripped of silk and satin, the dummy in the corner naked, the sewing machine idle?

'What will you do?'

'They say I should have the operation for cataract.'

'But your sewing? What will you live on?' Briskly she added, 'Of course Conal will take care of you.'

'His line of work is difficult of course.'

Then he could get himself a steady job, as a scaffy, if necessary, or a hospital porter and push stretchers in and out of lifts and along miles of grey corridors to the operating theatre. That was what Farquhar would have said if he had been here. He knew the unemployment figures as well as anyone but there was no need for anyone to be idle, not if they had the least bit of spunk in them. He himself would be prepared to sweep the streets before he would go on the dole. Emily did not suggest a steady job for Conal and neither did his mother. She said she knew he would never see her starve, he was a good boy, he was not averse to work, but could not be tied down, not nine-to-five, with some small-minded little man trying to make him conform. He never would conform. Emily supposed she could say that Camilla did not conform, or at least not to the standards of her upbringing, but of course she did stick quite closely to the mores of her new habitat. Whereas Conal ran with no pack, belonged to no group. It was pleasant to sit by the fire, drink whisky and talk about Conal. She said that Mrs McCreedy was lucky to have a son with whom she was so intimate. She had been close to her son until he was thirteen when Farquhar had insisted on sending him against her wishes and the boy's to public school. The school was in Edinburgh, but boarding was compulsory and so he had had to leave home just the same. It had seemed ridiculous. She used to stand in Queen Street and look down the hill at the spires of the school and think of him incarcerated there when he could have been in his own room at home, getting up in the morning to go to day school where he would have learned just as much and come home in the afternoons. Farquhar had said stupid things like making a man out of him, removing him from too much feminine influence. It was Farquhar's old school: that was the real reason, though he would not admit it. He might have been better if he had had more feminine influences in his life, she had told him in a rare outburst, and she did not count Davina and Elspeth whom she considered sexless and neuter. For the last remark she had to apologise and for a long time afterwards, when the sisters came to visit, Farquhar would raise his eyes across the table at her with a hint of reproach.

'Do you ever hear at all from your husband now, Mrs McCreedy?'

'Don't even know if he's alive or dead. Dead more than likely.

Probably fell off some pier dead drunk. Don't really care, not any more. Well, it's been a long time, hasn't it? Oh, he wasn't a bad fella, not wicked, you understand, just weak, but it gets terrible tedious living with a weak man so it does. He used to talk to himself, telling himself jokes, trying them out. He kept a joke book, wrote down anything he heard. I used to put cotton wool in my ears; better that than screaming. He sang a bit too, schmaltzy stuff, *Bless This House, Kathleen Mavourneen* and *The Mountains of Mourne*, that kind of thing. Enough to bring the tears to his eyes. And he did a bit of soft-shoe shuffle. All corn he was, soft corn. Couldn't blame him for drinking though, could you? You'd need something to lift you up after a five-minute burst of trying to get some of those fat-headed dolts to laugh. Sometimes his'd be the only laugh you could hear in the hall. I'm no good at acting myself, I was no help. Can you imagine what it's like having to laugh when you want to cry? Doesn't do much for the ego and his never was very hearty. He was one of ten kids from a Dublin slum, oh aye and a proper slum it was too, with his mother a shawlie, and his da living off his wits that were about as sharp as the backside of a shovel.'

So that was Conal's heritage, thought Emily, as she held out her glass for a refill. She fancied she saw part of it in him but doubted if his mother would care for her to voice that observation. She liked the sound of Mrs McCreedy's voice; it lilted and flowed, and in it she could discern the Irish accent, both North and South, overlaid with a suggestion of Scots. She felt lulled, might have sat on and on by the fire listening and nodding, inserting the occasional leading question, but she noticed that Mrs McCreedy was glancing at the clock on the mantelpiece. Conal must be expected shortly and she would have to get his tea. She had got his tea now for over thirty years, night after night. Her interest in the past had gone; her mind had moved to the present and the nice piece of haddock she had in the fridge for him. Emily forced herself to stand; she stretched and yawned and wondered if she could summon energy to drive.

She left, taking care as she went down the steep, dark stairs, keeping a hand on the clammy banister rail, putting each foot forward tentatively. Her ankle was still causing her a little trouble though was recovering nicely and would be fit to dance with again when called to. The lights had failed to come on and there were areas of such intense blackness that she had to pause and let her eyes adjust. One could so easily lose one's footing and fall, especially with a dram or two taken. On the second last flight she rounded a corner and went smack into an upcoming hurrying body. She gasped.

'Emily, is that you?'

'Conal!' She let her head fall forward in relief and come to rest against his shoulder.

He patted her hair and laughed, said he was sorry to have frightened her. They stood, bodies touching, she on the step above him.

'You'd better go. Your mother's getting your tea ready. Good luck tonight!'

'Give me a kiss for luck then, Emmie!'

She lifted her head and his mouth mets hers. His hands came up and cradled the sides of her face. How long the kiss lasted, she did not know, she lost track of time and place and Emily Mountjoy; she went into a kind of silken, sensuous swoon where nothing impinged other than the warmth of his body and the tremor of his lips. When he took his mouth away she could not get her breath. She leaned back against the wall. Louisa often went on about peak experiences. Perhaps she had just had one, although this was an experience she would not be able to discuss with Louisa. Conal was talking to her softly, saying he was sure he would have luck now, and he would look for her in the audience.

'I will play to you.'

She nodded.

He kissed her forehead quickly, then went upward, passing her, leaving her in the dim corner of the staircase. For fully five minutes she stood there allowing the hammering of her heart to quieten. What a silly old woman she was, trembling like a young girl after a first kiss! But that was what it had felt like.

She had to go and have a cup of tea before she felt capable of driving back to the Braid Hills.

'Where have you been, Emily?' asked Louisa.

'People are always asking me that! Farquhar, Camilla –'

Louisa said she was sorry but she had been worried, having expected her earlier. Emily threw a bag of frozen lamb casserole (factory prepared) into a pot of boiling water for Farquhar's dinner and went upstairs to bath and change. From the hall below, Louisa watched her with curiosity.

She soaked herself in a deep bath of fragrant water. When she stood on the mat and dried her body she regarded it with more affection than she had for a long time. She felt slimmer and even her skin seemed firmer and smoother. She sang to herself. 'I'm a rambler, I'm a gambler . . .'

A gentle knocking disturbed her. 'Emily? We'll need to be going soon or we'll be late.'

'Coming,' she sang.

From her wardrobe she selected a dress never worn but by no means new. It was of uncertain period, possibly Edwardian or just after, of crushed black velvet, with a plunging V-neckline and long wide sleeves. Carl had sold it to her since it was for the larger woman, few of whom frequented his shop. He had said she would look fabulous in it and she had allowed herself to be blackmailed into buying although, at the time, had had no intention of wearing it.

'What on earth have you got on?' asked Farquhar, looking up from his lamb casserole which Louisa had been kind enough to release from its bag for him.

'A dress. What do you think?'

She was not planning to go out in it, was she? Certainly, and why not?

'It's a beautiful dress, Emily.' Louisa sounded slightly stunned.

There was ice-cream in the fridge for his pudding, Emily told her husband, and some coffee in the pot he could reheat, and he should not bother to stay up as they would be late. They were planning to go and dance at Tiffany's to the Band of Gold. She had put a necklet of gold around her neck and a bangle of gold around her wrist.

Louisa was unusually quiet in the car. Emily chatted, telling her about Mrs McCreedy's husband. It explained a lot, didn't it, about Conal?

'I guess so. Emily, don't you think maybe you should go a bit easy on your husband? Well, I mean he's getting kind of fed up being left alone quite so much. Oh, forget it! I shouldn't have said that.'

Emily shook with laughter. She would have thought not indeed, especially since it was Louisa who had first encouraged her to start leading her own life, not of course that she was holding her responsible either. She was taking full responsibility for everything she was doing on her own shoulders. Anyway, for years Farquhar had left *her* alone.

'So it's sauce for the gander, eh?'

'I'm not thinking of it that way, Louisa. Not at all. I do not believe in retaliation.'

Conal did look for her the moment he came on stage. She saw his eyes search, find her, relax. She smiled back at him. Beside her Louisa moved restlessly.

Willy Loman's wife forgot her lines three times in the first act and had to be prompted, twice for one of them, but Conal carried on without showing a trace of disturbance although Emily knew it must be agonising for him underneath. She felt his agony like a wave flowing out to reach her. She felt each change of mood that he went through. It was as if they were connected with a current.

'He really should stop messing around with these amateurs,' said Louisa irritably, when the clapping had expired after the final curtain. She told him so too on their way to Tiffany's. And he told her what he had before. 'Oh, your bloody integrity! What's so special about that?' But he did not want to participate in TV soap operas, and why should he? 'There are other things besides that, you know. You're opting out, Conal. You're refusing the challenge that the professional theatre would bring to you. You might even develop more as an actor if you had to play soap opera or rep week after week. It would be good discipline.' How would she like to write articles on pimples and halitosis for women's magazines instead of chasing after her own obsessions? asked Conal. Would she find that a useful discipline? She would do it rather than starve, she said. He was not starving, he retaliated.

'No, because your mother keeps you.'

'Louisa!' cried Emily.

'My mother does not keep me.'

Louisa apologised though could not give up on him totally. There was the Traverse Theatre at the other end of the Grassmarket from him doing interesting and exciting new plays. There were people in the Highlands and Islands desperate for culture. There was much that he could do. His respite soon came : Louisa could not compete with the golden band.

He asked Emily to dance with him. He led her out on to the floor.

'Your dress is fantastic, Emmie. You look beautiful, like a ripe peach.'

She laughed. She knew that her skin glowed, and not from a hot flush.

Chapter Seven

IT was one of Emily's mornings at the charity shop. After a late night she had been tempted to ring and plead indisposition but her sense of duty forged through years of habit pushed her to go, even though her absence would scarcely have caused a ripple through the old clothes and she could not deceive herself that she would be doing much to help alleviate the sufferings of the world. The shops served two purposes: they recycled second-hand goods cheaply and gave some women something to do.

The other two women who were on with her that morning had already arrived and were drinking tea. They had the *Scotsman* opened up across the counter and were shaking their heads over it. For a second Emily almost turned and ran but hesitated a second too long and once they had lifted their eyes to her face it was too late to go.

She went through to the back room and took off her coat.

'Terrible the things they print even in here nowadays. It's sunk almost as low as the gutter press. If it weren't for the births, marriages and deaths I wouldn't dream of taking it.'

Emily poured herself a cup of tea.

'It's the Scottish Nationalists, you know.'

'Really?'

'Oh yes! No question.'

And how was Mrs Mountjoy this morning? They folded up the newspaper. And how was she getting along with her little blind dressmaker? She regretted greatly ever having told them about Mrs McCreedy and only had to ease the boredom of a morning in which the door had opened but twice and her companions had gone on about the lack of decent service nowadays. Plumbers said they'd call, you stayed in and they never arrived. You used to be able to get all sorts of little jobs done, mending, odd bits of sewing, but unfortunately that sort of person seemed to have died off and couldn't be replaced. So what about this Mrs McCreedy? they asked now. Were her charges reasonable? They could both use new outfits and prices in the shops were shocking these days.

'You have to be a plumber or a typist to afford them.'

'It is a fact, Mrs Smiley.'

'Rubbish,' said Mrs Mountjoy.

The two women looked at one another, one lifted the *Scotsman*, the other gathered up the dirty cups.

'We'd better get to work then, ladies.'

Emily put a bundle of Warwick Deepings and Marie Corellis into the shelf beside a collection of soiled Readers Digests. Her eye was arrested by a title. *The Rosary* by Florence L. Barclay. How she had enjoyed that when she was sixteen! She opened the pages, smelled the familiar smell of old books and pressed it to her nose. The story of the beautiful young painter with a strong sense of aesthetic appreciation falling in love with a woman who was so ugly one could almost not bear to look at her face. She had known that she could not inflict such ugliness on a man of such heightened sensitivity and so had nobly removed herself. But the dilemma was solved by him being blinded, and they were able to live happily ever after. Luckily she'd had a beautiful voice. Emily laughed. The ladies eyed one another.

'I'll buy this myself. Twenty pence. Think I can afford that.'

'There are one or two things I'd like to show you through the back, Mrs Smiley.'

'Certainly, Mrs Crichton.'

They moved into the back room leaving the door ajar since there were too many objects obstructing for it to be closed. Their voices rose and fell on various levels of murmuring. They thought she was going a little odd, it might be her time of life of course, but even so! And what a good family she was from, or anyway married into; Farquhar Mountjoy was highly regarded and his sisters were simply delightful women. They looked back from the doorway, arching their narrow backs. Mrs Mountjoy was sitting on the floor reading.

And then her awful daughter arrived. That was just about the last straw, said Mrs Smiley, moving out into the shop for she did not trust the girl, no matter who her father was. Some of that Stockbridge colony really were odd, gave you the creeps they did, with their greasy hair and old clothes. Camilla came in most weeks to see what they had; she would buy up a few things and then go and sell them at double the price in her own shop which was little better than the old rag-and-bone type establishments you used to get in the Cowgate. Not that they could do anything about her doubling the price: if people were fool enough to pay it that was up to them.

'Hi, Ma!'

Emily was chuckling. 'You should read this, Camilla. It really is funny.'

Camilla began to rake amongst the rack of clothes wrinkling her nose at the Crimplene suits and dresses. The women watched her closely, whilst folding and refolding some knitted baby rompers.

'Got any evening gear?'

'We don't like customers to handle them themselves but we can show a few things to you, if you wish.'

Camilla made a face as Mrs Crichton went to unlock a cupboard in the corner. She brought back four or five long dresses over her arm. Camilla put out her hand to touch the cloth.

'Please. If you don't mind.'

'My hands are clean. My mum taught me to wash them after I go to the loo, you know.'

Emily left *The Rosary* and got up to ease the situation. She took the matter into her own hands, literally, for Mrs Smiley could hardly object to letting her hold the dress in question. It was made of violet crêpe and generously bedecked with sequins. Quite dreadful, thought Emily, as she held it up for her daughter to admire. Mrs Smiley stayed close to the action and even Mrs Crichton, whilst continuing to fold rompers, kept an eye on what was going on.

'I'll take it,' said Camilla, digging out her purse from a Greek bag which was suspended from her waist on a string. 'How much?'

Emily turned over the ticket. 'Four pounds.'

'Four pounds?' said Mrs Smiley. 'I'm sure it can't be as little as that, Mrs Mountjoy. Are you sure it's not seven?' She took the ticket between her finger and thumb. 'I rather think it is.

What do you say, Mrs Crichton? It looks like your handwriting.'

Mrs Crichton put on her reading glasses and peered at the ticket. She frowned. 'Yes, I rather think it is, Mrs Smiley. Seven pounds.'

'It's four,' said Mrs Mountjoy clearly. 'I wrote the ticket myself and Mrs Donaldson decided the price. You can ask her.'

They murmured. No need to do that. They would take Mrs Mountjoy's word, any time.

'But it really *should* have been seven, I think,' said Mrs Smiley.

'It is really rather a steal at the price,' said Mrs Crichton.

'I'm not proposing to steal anything,' said Camilla. 'I'm going to give you good honest-to-God cash for it.' She took four well-used pound notes and held them out to Mrs Smiley.

Mrs Smiley did not take them. She decided there were times when one should speak one's mind and Mrs Crichton was quite in agreement when they discussed it later. Society would not be in such a dreadful state if people did make a stand once in a while.

'We know that you are going to go and sell this garment at a profit, and that is not what we are here for. We would like you to know that we disapprove on moral grounds.'

'But your husband owns a bloody biscuit factory. Talk about capitalism and making a profit there !'

'What my husband sells is none of your business.'

'And what I sell is none of yours.'

'The dress is no longer for sale. We are withdrawing it.'

Mrs Crichton nodded. They stood shoulder to shoulder. Mrs Mountjoy still held the purple dress.

'It's against the law,' she said. 'If you offer something for sale you've got to sell it at the price marked.'

'We are a charity, not a commercial concern.'

'We are still dealing commercially. And we are not outside the law. The dress is for sale at four pounds, Camilla.'

Camilla gave her mother the money and in exchange received the purple dress.

'I think that this has been a most unfortunate incident, Mrs Mountjoy,' said Mrs Crichton.

'I heartily agree. Just a minute, Camilla, I'm coming with you.' She was putting on her fur coat watched by the two women. 'Oh, before I forget – my twenty p.' She laid the coins on the counter and lifted the book. 'I have to say that it is with great relief I am giving up my good works. The good that we think we do is mainly for ourselves, you know.'

Camilla, hugging the purple sequined dress to her chest, collapsed outside the door in gusts of laughter. The women had come to the door and were peering out, one on either side of the 'OPEN' sign.

'You were wild.' Camilla dried her eyes on the dress. 'Wait till I tell Carl! He always did say you were capable of surprising us.' But Carl was not in the shop when they got there. A note stuck to the door said: 'Back in ten minutes'. Camilla removed it and they went inside. She put the piece of paper with a pile of others which said 'Back at two-thirty', 'Back at four'. Most contingencies were catered for. It saved a lot of writing, said Camilla, and half the time they couldn't find paper to write on anyway.

Emily had a look around the stock, most of which looked the same as it had before, although Camilla said they had lots of new stuff in. She made coffee and they drank it in front of the oil heater which gave off unappetising fumes. The place smelt and felt damp and Emily worried about Camilla getting rheumatism. She was looking very pale and had heavy blue rings beneath her eyes.

'Are you feeling all right, dear?'

'I'm fine.' Her reply was edged with aggression.

Carl did not come back in ten minutes or in thirty. Camilla kept looking at the street.

'Where can he be?'

'Probably screwing a red-haired bitch who lives round the corner.'

'Camilla!'

'Sorry. I keep forgetting. Well, it's difficult, nobody thinks anything – '

'It's not your language that upsets me. It's the thought that Carl might be unfaithful to you.'

'There's no might. He is.'

'And don't you mind?'

'Of course I mind. I mind like crazy. I mind like I could go and scrape her eyeballs out. And the same goes for the black-haired bitch that lives across the road. You can see her standing in front of her window undressing.'

'There's more than one?'

Camilla said to forget it, she shouldn't have told her mother, she had just let it slip out and there was no point in telling her to leave him since she had no intention of doing it. 'He doesn't like me to be possessive, says he needs to feel free to wander every now and then and that he'll always come back.'

'So it's to be all on his terms? He can have his fun when he wants it.'

'I can have it off with anyone I fancy too. But I don't fancy anyone but Carl. Oh, Christ!' She began to cry. Large tears rolled down her face and Emily got up thinking how young and vulnerable the child looked and how ill-equipped she was to cope with such a life. But who was equipped for any life? Coping came through experience, sometimes. She put her arms round the thin shoulders and for a moment Camilla cried against her bosom, as he did when she was small.

The door jangled open and Camilla leapt back snuffling.

'What's going on?' asked Carl.

'I might ask you that. If I was to look I might find a few red hairs on you.'

Camilla lacked diplomacy, thought Emily; she would spend all day atoning for her sharp words.

'I was up at the sale buying a load of smelly old fur coats if you want to know. Bloody laugh a minute that was, scrambling with a lot of old bags. They're out on the pavement.'

As they looked up at the heap of fur a large thin dog came along and lifted its leg to eject a stream of yellow liquid. With a yell Carl dashed back up the steps and returned with the pile. They dripped all over the shop, on to Camilla's feet and a collection of satin shoes and the purple crêpe dress. Emily decided it was time to leave. She was going on a tour of the second-hand bookshops which she found much more *sympathique* places to browse in than second-hand clothes shops. She hated other people's stale odours and the sight of their stains offended her sensibilities. Of course Camilla attributed that to her being a member of the bourgeoisie. As she walked along the road, she sang softly to herself. She felt liberated now that she had freed herself from her good works. To compensate she would double her usual amount in the tin when people came round collecting. A conscience sop. No matter what one did one could never do anything very effective to help, not unless one went into the thick of a situation, dragged children out of blitzed burning houses, bound up their wounds, cradled them in one's arms and uttered reassuring lies to quieten their terror. If she were to go she would get in the way, become one of the dead or wounded and therefore just an added nuisance. No, she had better stay in Edinburgh and help Louisa in her search for American women in Scotland and take bread and cheese to her daughter. For her husband she could not do much, not now; to him she had given all she had to give. And then there was Conal. She did not know yet what she could give there.

He was in the first bookshop she went in to in Dundas Street. He was looking at a book on Sean O'Casey.

'I was just wishing I was more adventurous,' she said. 'Like Freya Stark, or some of those nineteenth-century women who travelled in wild places doing the most incredible things with total faith in themselves and what they were doing.'

He smiled. He thought that she was not unadventurous.

She sighted a two-volume biography of Emily Dickinson and swooped down on it with a cry of triumph. She purchased it. They left the shop together.

'And now let me take you to lunch. It's to be my treat, so no arguing!' She wanted to take him to Cramond to eat at the inn and afterwards they could walk along the foreshore. She had her car nearby. 'That's if you can bear to leave the city for a couple of hours?'

With her he could leave it for a couple of days, he said. Or weeks. They lingered over lunch, drinking wine with their food, finishing with coffee and liqueurs. She bought him a large fat cigar. What a wonderful idea this had been, he said. She thought of Louisa eating a salami sandwich at the kitchen table but that was Louisa's affair.

'Do you ever feel guilt, Conal?'

'Of course. Who doesn't?'

'But you are not burdened with it?'

Mockingly, he said he could always go to confession if the sin was large enough, but who was to say which sins were serious and which trifling? It depended on their effects on others, he supposed. Emily rather wished she had been born Catholic, she knew she could never become one, not take the conscious decision, but if it had been taken for her at birth she thought she could have found the religion to her liking.

'Do you feel guilty about things, Emily?'

'Not much, no. Not nowadays. That is the strange thing. But I keep feeling that I should.'

That made him laugh.

They finished their Drambuie and went to walk along the promenade and look at the sail boats which were laid up for the winter. The wind coming off the Firth was strong and cold. She felt as if it was cleaning out her lungs and recharging her batteries. After they had gone a few yards he reached out for her hand and took it. He slipped off her beaver mitt and put his hand and hers entwined together into the depths of his big tweed pocket.

'That's better. Skin is such lovely stuff, a shame not to be able to feel it.'

It was one of the days that Elspeth and Davina chose to walk from Queensferry to Cramond. It was a favourite walk of theirs and they were great believers in taking plenty of exercise in the fresh air, summer or winter. Edinburgh being the kind of place that it was – not too large, and where many circles interlocked and everyone knew so many of the same people – Emily half expected that on her stroll with Conal she would meet someone she knew or who knew her in some category or other. But she had not bargained for a meeting with her sisters-in-law. They rounded a bend and there they were, coming towards them in belted mackintoshes and woollen headscarves; and as soon as she saw them she cursed herself for having forgotten their addiction to Cramond. They went everywhere the wind was cold.

They had to stop. She pulled her hand from Conal's pocket. It looked pink and naked beside its fur-clad partner. From his other pocket protruded her second mitt. She made the introductions and Conal talked of the charms of Cramond and complimented the ladies on having walked all the way from Queensferry in such a bitter wind.

'Davina and Elspeth have great stamina,' said Emily.

They coughed behind their cuffs. They must be getting on their way, but they would see her this evening, wouldn't they? She looked blank. She was remembering that she and Farquhar were coming to them for dinner? Seven-thirty for eight, as usual. They nodded to Conal, then passed on in their tightly laced-up brogues, their backs held straight. They did not look back.

'Such restraint,' murmured Emily.

She and Conal stayed around the corner long enough to give them time to get clear before they themselves turned back. He put his arms around her to protect her from the wind, and as they waited he rocked her a little.

'Will they tell your husband?'

She thought almost certainly not, since they would find it vulgar to have to speak of such things, but she did not care if they did.

'I love you for that.'

She looked up at him and he kissed her. Other people passed, men with dogs, men and women alone, men on bicycles – amazing how much traffic for a winter afternoon – but she was not conscious of them, except as vague, moving blurs. They kissed again and again. They kissed until she gasped and laughed. He put his hands inside the thick warmth of her coat and caressed her breasts. She was so warm and soft that he wanted to drown in her.

It began to rain and they allowed the soft drops to moisten their heads and faces and run between their lips, but then the shower swelled to a downpour and they had to run, clutching hands, he pulling her, to the shelter of the car. They bundled themselves inside. They were soaking wet. They looked like drookit hens, he said. Simultaneously, they turned to one another and laughed. They laughed so easily. This must be madness, she decided, but if it was, preferred it to sanity.

'So I won't see you until tomorrow?' He made it sound like

an eternity. He held on to her hands, would not let her start the engine and make the first move that would take them back to Edinburgh. The wind and rain lashed the outside of the car making for them inside a warm isolated nest. Like his mother's room must be in a storm, except that she had a fire to glow and spark. But they had no need of a fire, thought Emily; they were warm, resting against one another, taking heat from the other's body. She cradled him in her arms, his head resting against her breast.

At length, the rain slackened. A man passed their car casting a glance in at them as he went. It was time to go.

She had to drop Conal in the Grassmarket and move on for the black and yellow traffic wardens were buzzing close by, licking the ends of their biros and writing tickets. He jumped out quickly and as she turned right she saw, from the corner of her eye, a woman emerged from the McCreedys' stair. The woman knew Conal and greeted him warmly. The impression was brief but enough to trouble, to start up wriggles of doubt. Was this a woman he was dallying with too? Was he dallying with her? She did not believe it! She could hear Mrs Seton's voice. You can't trust these people, actors are all the same, turning on the charm when it suits them, playing roles. It was thus she had spoken of Conal yesterday when she had called to return a magazine and Mrs Mountjoy had said what an interesting and talented young man he seemed to be, oh not that she knew him very well of course. She found that she had an overwhelming desire to talk about him, directly or indirectly. She could not believe he was playing with her. But whether he was or not, where was it all leading? She braked at a red light. She felt the old hot flush rising from the cleft between her breasts, surging up her neck to her face. He had put his hands down there, had set her flesh singing. And she had enjoyed it. Was she shameless? That was what Farquhar would say, and Davina and Elspeth, and the two women in the charity shop. Someone was tooting at her. The light was green. She went ahead.

Louisa was giving Farquhar tea and hot buttered toast in the kitchen. He had come home early from the office, having been troubled by a bit of a stomach upset since morning. Immediately,

Emily was solicitous, but there was nothing for her to do, he said, Louisa had been most kind, and no, it was not serious enough for them to call off Davina and Elspeth's dinner party. It would not do to let them down especially as they were having the Craig Patersons with them.

'The Craig Patersons? Oh no!'

'I know that she is a bit much but Craig is one of my oldest friends.'

'You have a lot of close friends, Mr Mountjoy,' said Louisa. 'You've kept them all from childhood onward whereas I –' She shrugged.

'But you Americans do tend to move around a lot. And we Scots –'

'We Edinburghers,' corrected Emily.

He looked at her.

'A lot of Scots travel all over the place. But I think the people of Edinburgh, particularly the kind of people that Farquhar knows, in law, medicine, merchant banking and so forth, tend to hold fast to their own territory.'

'I think it must be marvellous to hold fast to one's territory,' said Louisa. 'To have roots that go deep down and hold you fast when the storms gather.'

'You see, Emily, even Louisa concedes the need for some conservatism, as well as conservation.'

She allowed him to have the last word in the exchange, not feeling a need to have it herself. Although Louisa spoke in an envious way of people with roots Emily wondered how she would like to find herself rooted to one spot. Could she cope with it after all those years of roaming, and did the roaming come from some deep need or was it simply a habit, a disease caught from her father? Emily pondered, whilst Louisa and Farquhar finished off a conversation they had begun before she came in, but arrived at no conclusion. Nor did she think that Louisa would either if she were to ponder herself.

Farquhar went upstairs to change.

'You know, he's not such a stuffed old shirt, Emily.'

'You think I've misrepresented him?'

Louisa wouldn't say that exactly but she had spent a pleasant hour with him in which he had told her something about Scots law and the ways in which it differed from English.

'How nice,' said Emily. And now she had to hurry and get herself ready for her sisters-in-law.

They would have to use her car, said Farquhar, as his own was in the garage. There was something wrong with the gear box. But he would drive; he never liked to be a passenger, especially when his wife was the driver. He tutted as he reversed the car into the street, complaining that she was messing up the clutch. She really was a hashy driver. Docilely, she admitted it, had no leg to stand on, as it were, so did not try to defend herself on that charge. She hated machines and if ever she was to go and live in the centre of the city she would surrender her car at once and go everywhere by foot, or bicycle.

'What are you smiling about?'

'Nothing, dear.'

He retrieved a handkerchief from beneath the brake. It was large, and obviously a man's handkerchief. In the corner there was an initial that was not the letter F.

'Whose is this, Emily?'

She took it from him. 'Does it matter, Farquhar? Someone must have dropped it.'

They shot across the intersection, narrowly missing a head-on collision with a car which had right of way.

'Are you sure your stomach's all right, dear? Perhaps you'd like me to drive?'

But he was not that ill. He stopped for a moment by the side of the road and wiped the sweat from his brow with the handkerchief which his wife put into his hand.

Dinner was served on silver platters at the Misses Mountjoys. The food was good and of delicate flavour but there was never enough of it for Elspeth and Davina judged everyone's appetites by their own and Emily came home feeling hungry. She always came home feeling paralysed with cold too: the flames licking at the few knobs of coal in the grate made little impact on the high room. As she fiddled with a tiny trout which was the main course she longed for a hunk of French bread, a thick wedge of Camembert, a litre of rough red wine, and a blast of hot dry air. How she would love to go to France with Conal, to the Lot and Garonne, or the Auvergne, stay in small hotels and eat in *routier* restaurants, sitting down before steaming tureens of soup and platters of veal stew.

'You and Farquhar are off to Corfu in May, I hear, Emily?' Jacynth Paterson was addressing her. 'Lucky you!' They had just come back from Barbados which she had talked about over the sherry and soup without ceasing. Her talk was unstoppable, like a nervous twitch.

'I may go to France instead.'

'France?' Farquhar frowned. 'You've not said anything about wanting to go to France. Besides, we're booked for Corfu.'

Emily did not have to answer, for Jacynth did, telling of the time they went to Corfu, of the times they had been everywhere. She was like a talking travel writer, only that her judgment was of no value, being totally subjective, confined to whether she had liked the people at the next table and if the temperature of the swimming pool had been to her liking. The last hotel they'd stayed in had had a terrible view. Of a building site. A room with a view was very important whilst on holiday, intercepted Emily, but only for the space of that brief comment. She saw herself with Conal, shutters thrown back against white walls, leaning out listening to the cicadas, watching a lizard snake along the wall; and down below, in the valley, the corn and sunflowers would be growing high and the canteloupes giving off a sweet aromatic smell. She and Farquhar had rented a house on the Lot one summer, taking Camilla; it had been in a small hamlet beside a Renaissance church and every day at midday an ancient peasant woman in a black dress and straw hat had come to toll the bell twelve times. Perhaps it might be possible to rent that house again. When she went home she would look in Farquhar's files and see if she could find the address. What was she thinking of? Was it even a possibility to go to France with Conal, stay in the same house with him, eat with him, sleep with him? Her hand shook and she spilt her wine right across the sisters' cream-coloured damask cloth. Fortunately it was white wine, unlikely to stain, as Elspeth said, sending her perturbed glances as she mopped up the damage and put a small cloth beneath the wet patch.

Emily was unaware of what evolved during the rest of the evening's conversation — nothing different, to judge from Farquhar's grumbling on the way home — for in her mind there was only one theme running. She must get to France with Conal.

Chapter Eight

FARQUHAR MOUNTJOY was meticulous in the keeping of records. It was possible to look back to 1955 and find what the gas bill had been for the second quarter and the name of the plumber who had mended the blocked drain. Under the file marked 'Holidays' Emily easily found the address she was seeking. Beneath it he had written the comments : sound house, clean, good views, dining-room chairs uncomfortable, rather isolated. The owner of the property lived in Cheshire, and there was a telephone number supplied. If she remembered rightly they had got it from an advertisement in the *Sunday Times*.

She shut herself up in the study after Farquhar had gone to work. She said that she was just making a tentative enquiry and wanted to know if they were booked up over the spring months. The woman said that the house was free any time from now until the beginning of June when the season started up properly. It would not be over-warm there at the moment, of course, especially at night, but the fireplaces did work in the sitting room and there were masses of logs in the old cowshed. She rambled on about the log-sawing enthusiasm of her husband and son. It would be rather nice to sit by log fires in the evening, said Emily, seeing them ensconced in the deep settee, inhaling scented woodsmoke, reaching out for another glass of the local wine. They talked for a long time on the joys of the French countryside and its cuisine until the woman said, 'Hey, this must be costing you a fortune. It's the peak time.' Emily promised to make contact again when her plans were more definite. She consulted a calendar, ticking off the next couple of weeks in her mind, for Conal had his O'Casey to do, but after that he had nothing on for a while as far as she knew. He tended to be vague about his plans, in which she rejoiced, for she already had one man in her life who lived a cut-

and-dried existence. Conal, Micawber-like, awaited with san-guinity for things to turn up. After making rings around certain dates on the calendar she rang up to enquire about insurance cover for taking her car abroad. She felt like a scheming woman, she who had only schemed but once before. The thought of that sobered her slightly. It too had involved a man. But that was a long time ago and the circumstances had been quite different.

That time was in her mind again, though, today, and she knew it was because of Conal. That man then had been around the age Conal must be now, and she herself much younger, not yet twenty, a student immersed in Virginia Woolf and D. H. Lawrence. She went downtown intending to go to the Central Library on a mission for Louisa, but instead found herself wander-ing up Forrest Road and down Lauriston Place towards the Art College. He had been a mature student there, had come to do a post-graduate course from abroad. He had come from a different culture, a different climate. It was his exoticism that had drawn her in the first instance. He had lived in one scruffy, paint-spattered room on a top floor facing north near the college. The room had always been cold but he had liked it because of the light. She had found it cold standing there naked, hour after hour, and he had shouted at her if she as much as changed the angle of an elbow. He could be fierce. She had never imagined that she would be prepared to expose her body for a man to paint. But this man had had a strange effect on her. As Conal did. Yes, she was willing to admit that, to herself.

She turned into the tenement stair. Not that he would still be there of course. He had gone back to Trinidad years ago. He was black; black as the coal-scuttle, said her father after he had seen them walking across the Meadows together, her white hand in his dark one. The effect on her father had been like that of an electric shock; he had had to sit down sharply on one of the benches, and she had run to him terrified that she might have killed him. He had not been able to speak but he had held up his hand. Keep back!

The stair looked no different, was still a place where students holed up cheaply and the landlords made the minimum of repairs. On every door was a card with a list of names. At the top she paused to recover her breath. She looked at his old door and read the names. The names of strangers who would be here today and gone tomorrow; they were not part of the strata that included the Mountjoys, Jamieson-Browns and Craig Robertsons.

The door opened suddenly, startling her. A young man was coming out, books under his arm. Was she looking for somebody? Stammering, blushing, she asked if anyone of her friend's name lived there, but he shook his head, said he'd never heard that name, called back into the flat to ask if someone inside had heard it either. A girl came out of a room, trailing a long skirt over the dusty linoleum. It didn't matter, said Emily Mountjoy, backing away; it was a long time ago, it had just been a chance . . .

'Come in,' said the girl. 'I'll see if Penny's heard of him.'

Emily went inside. At once his face came back, so long forgotten; obliterated from memory, she had thought. She saw his eyes, large, dark, sometimes smiling, sometimes bad-tempered when his work was going badly. His temper could rise like a volcano. She had not been prepared for that, having come from a well-regulated family which had been taught that it was bad-mannered to raise the voice above a certain pitch. Everything about him had set her senses tingling. She saw his teeth so white against his skin, heard his laugh, deep, rumbling from the pit of his belly, felt the heat of his hands when he put them on her shoulders.

Penny was living in his room. She was lying on the bed reading Kurt Vonnegut. The walls were still the same dark red. It seemed unbelievable. After more than thirty years! She exclaimed aloud. The two girls who had not been born then were only mildly interested or surprised. As far as they were concerned the place had been the way it was since the Dark Ages. The room was a room was a dump and the paper was peeling off the walls and the mice came out at nights in battalions. They had even been known to scuttle over Penny's bed; she had wakened one night and found one nibbling her ear. Emily commiserated; she could not remember if mice had been a problem in her day. Possibly, but he would never have bothered to mention them. She had never spent a night here; in those days it was inconceivable to spend a night away from home without parents asking fifth-degree questions. To sleep with a man was to be labelled a whore. And to sleep with a black man would in her father's eyes be enough to justify being cast into hell.

'Fancy a coffee?' asked Penny. 'The water's boiled.'

That would be nice, she said. Loosening her coat, she sat down on the bed, and looked at the red wall. He used to pose her against the wall, said her skin looked good set off by the colour. She remembered how the goosepimples used to rise on the upper part of her arms and after a bit she would start to shiver and he would come and run his hands all over her body and warm her until she tingled.

'I once had a boyfriend who lived here,' she told the girls.

'You didn't marry him though?'

'No.'

Most boyfriends one didn't marry after all, said the other girl. She was living with a bloke at the moment but she expected they'd break up after they graduated.

'You're lucky you can live together. In my day –'

They couldn't imagine their mothers saying that; they had to pretend they shared the flat only with other girls.

'I think it's a definite improvement. Much more honest.'

'Did you sleep with your boyfriend?' It was a question they asked easily: there was no impertinence in it, or even great curiosity.

She nodded. Yes, she had, and they were the first people she had ever admitted it to, bar one, who did not count in the same way. Strange to admit such a personal thing to strangers, but perhaps it was not. She had not even told Louisa about him, or Conal. But she might tell Conal when they went to France.

'Did you go around with him for a long time?'

'A year. He was an artist. A West Indian.'

That interested them; even they could realise that thirty years ago it must have posed problems for her. Oh indeed, she said, allowing Penny to help her ease her fur coat off her shoulders. They had met at a club called International House, now defunct. The premises had been on the corner of Princes and Castle Street and had had a marvellous view looking right out on to the castle. It had been full of Norwegians and Nigerians and Egyptians, as well as quite a number of Scots too. She laughed, leaned back against the wall. She had had a lot of fun there, had enjoyed the mixing of the races. Of course her family hadn't known she'd gone; they regarded the place with strong suspicion, seemed to think it was some kind of sink of iniquity where girls from good Scottish families were sold into slavery and opium was peddled. And maybe these things had gone on: she wouldn't have known, was very innocent in those days. She had first been taken along by a fellow student, a Malaysian girl from Singapore who was going round with a Sudanese doctor. They went to play table tennis, she and the Malaysian girl, one afternoon, and after a bit, as they were playing, she became aware of a pair of eyes watching her. He had eyes like that: you felt them even on your back. She turned, missed her shot, and saw him for the first time. He was leaning against the wall. After that she played badly, soon gave up. When they went upstairs to have a drink she found him at her elbow leaning on the bar. 'You move beautifully,' he said. She laughed now. Wasn't that incredible? And these days she moved like an elephant! Nonsense, said Penny, she moved very gracefully; she herself had noticed it the moment she came into the room.

'So that was the beginning of it?'

He followed her everywhere, up and down Middle Meadow Walk, around the Old Quad, down the Mound, into the club, saying he must paint her. He *would* paint her. She couldn't take him seriously, didn't want to, was afraid. Because of his strangeness, she supposed. And yet she was attracted by it too. When she went to the dance at the club on a Saturday night he was already there, waiting. 'That was the end of it really. The end of my resistance!' As soon as she danced with him, felt the rhythm of his body against hers, she knew that there was no point in pretending any longer. They left the dance early, came back here to his room. She trembled with excitement, but was no longer afraid. He could be such a gentle man. He was gentle.

Penny sighed. For a moment they were quiet, all three each locked into her separate thoughts. And then Emily became brisk.

'I must go.' She reached for her coat. She was sure they had work to do and they had been very kind to entertain her. Come

again, they said, but she knew she would not. She thanked them
for the coffee, took a last look at the red room, and walked back
down the stairs. She did not approve of nostalgia trips, had always
fought against indulging herself, but this particular one did not
seem to have harmed her. On the contrary, it had warmed her,
made her feel that that year was still a part of her and that not
all had been thrown away. For at least five years after he had
returned to Trinidad she had not been able to think of him without pain. She thought about him long after she was married to
Farquhar. You are lucky to have such a man as Farquhar Mountjoy as your husband, said her family, who were now all dead and
gone and not in a position to care any longer if she was married
to a black man. Not that *he* had wanted to marry her. He was
going to go home and marry his second cousin : that way the race
would be unpolluted, he said. Much better that way. Who would
want a coffee-coloured child? She had. She had stood in the red
room and wept and railed at him but he would not be moved.
He had promised her nothing and that she was not able to deny.
His honesty could not be called into question; hers might have
been. She had schemed to have that man, had wanted him
passionately, had loved his earthiness and vigour, his sudden
storms, his wholehearted, infectious laugh. And she had loved his
lack of puritanism and inhibition. She had loved him for not being
Farquhar Mountjoy. In him she had seen a chance to break
what appeared to be her predestined pattern. And when that bid
collapsed and she was left exhausted there seemed nothing else to
do but get rid of the coffee-coloured foetus in her womb and allow
herself to be claimed by Farquhar Mountjoy, have him put five
diamonds around the fourth finger of her left hand, and in due
course a solid gold band. She almost did not care. So be it. That
was how she felt as she walked up the aisle of St Giles Cathedral
in white lace masquerading as a virgin. No one in the whole
congregation knew her secret, could guess the tumultuous thoughts
passing to and fro through her mind. We none of us know much
of what the other is thinking, she had thought, as she had stood
beside the young man in morning suit listening to him repeat his
vows. Perhaps he too would have liked to cut and run and throw
his top hat over the steeple. Before her moment of answering she

had paused. The pause had seemed like one of all eternity and she had thought she would have to turn, to face the congregation, and put her back to the altar. I, Emily Grace . . . As soon as she said the words she could hear the ripple run through the congregation. All brides were nervous of course, nothing unusual in a minute or two's hesitation. When the words were said the tumult within her settled, her life was set on a new course, and she smiled at Farquhar Mountjoy, her lawfully wedded husband. It would probably not have worked anyway, to be the white wife of a black man, with a brown child, in a foreign land. Too much would have been stacked against them. All for the best in the end. Edinburgh was familiar; nothing too drastic could happen to her here.

The city most certainly was familiar; every spire and rooftop, street and vennel, was carved into her mind even though she had not looked at them closely for a long time. All the years of her married life, driving around town in her little car, she had seen the traffic and the intersections of the roads, had thought about turning right and left or going straight on; now she felt possessed of a new set of eyes, found that she was looking as she used to do with him when they walked for hour after hour through the streets, going down flights of steps from the ridge of the High Street to drop to the level below, stopping to look at the tall backlands. It had all been so new for him, in line, colour, lifestyle. He immersed himself in it wanting to extract from this environment every drop of its essence. She had been a part of that essence for him, she realised, she had been within the framework, belonging here and nowhere else. He had not considered that she could be removed from it and transported. And so he had turned his back on her and gone, leaving his long shadow to lie across her life.

Without thinking, she had turned down Candlemaker Row. Without consciously thinking, she corrected herself. She stopped to look in an antique shop window and saw, propped against the side wall, a mirror in the Art Nouveau style. Miraculously, the shop was open.

The mirror was of beaten silver with four blue beads set within the frame. It was the genuine article, said the man, in perfect condition. In the glass she saw herself smiling. The man was going on about Art Nouveau and the Glasgow school and how difficult it was to get the real stuff nowadays: that was why the price was a little stiff.

'I'll take it.'

He took it from her to wrap. 'You collect Art Nouveau?'

'A friend of mine does.'

He had another little thing in the back shop, a brass tray, beautifully decorated. Twenty pounds. A man was coming in to see it in the afternoon, was almost certain to want it, but if she was interested he'd let her have the first chance.

Carrying the two parcels, she made her way up the Grassmarket. The mirror was heavy so she walked carefully balancing the edge of it against her hip. She decided she would go and sit in a café and hope that Conal might come by on his way to or from the library. He went most days.

Sitting in the window, she drank two cups of coffee and ate one piece of cake, resisting a second, and watched the passers-by, the meths men and the students and the early tourists. And then, almost when she had given up, Conal came, the sleeve of his coat brushing the window on the other side. She rose to call his name. But he was not alone. He was walking with a woman, the one she had seen come out of his stair the day before.

She ran to the door bumping tables as she went. They were walking, Conal and the woman, arm-in-arm. She saw them go into the Beehive restaurant two doors along. It was lunchtime.

'You've left two parcels,' a young man was calling to her. She took them from his hands.

She stood in the middle of the Grassmarket, her parcels clasped to her stomach, and did not know where to go next. A taxi was coming. Raising a hand to hail it, she dropped the larger parcel. The one containing the mirror. She heard the thud as it hit the ground.

When she got home she went straight up to her room without removing her shoes or fur coat and undid the parcel with fingers that fumbled and struggled with the string. The glass was splintered right across. Seven years bad luck. No, she did not believe in such superstitions. She would not! she cried out loud. But the beautiful mirror was no longer perfect. She sat down on the velvet-pile carpet and wept.

'Emily?' Louisa was tapping, calling, opening the door a crack to see what was the matter. Could she come in? She came. She saw the mirror and understood at once for whom it had been bought.

'I just saw it and thought he would like it,' said Emily helplessly, wondering how much more foolish it was possible to be. Couldn't she have learned over the years when to stand back? Or had she stood back for so long that she could not cope with coming forward?

'It's a real shame,' said Louisa, again.

'I could always get the glass replaced, I suppose,' said Emily, and then remembered the woman on Conal's arm. She got up and put her purchases into the back of a cupboard and turned the key.

'Forget it, Louisa. I am just a silly old woman.'

The telephone rang when they were finishing lunch.

'Emily,' said Conal, 'shall I see you this evening? Are you and Louisa coming to the theatre?'

'I'm afraid not. I have another engagement.'

He asked what was the matter and she said that nothing was, and he said that she sounded different, different from yesterday at Cramond, and so they went on for a few minutes, sterilely revolving around one another with words and phrases.

'Have I offended you, Emily? Tell me please if I have! Did I do something yesterday that upset you?'

She had never been good at holding in, always in the end did come out with her resentment. She made him laugh. That woman meant nothing to him! She was a friend of his mother's, one of her customers, and they were merely going for a drink together. Emily felt it was ridiculous of her to object at all, knowing she had no right to; and yet she had suffered agonies of jealousy when she had seen him arm-in-arm with another woman. Jealousy was such an unattractive vice.

'Come and meet me now, Emily.'

She told Louisa she was going out and went, taking the brass tray with her.

Conal thought the tray exquisite. He scolded her for spending money on him. He had spent nothing on her, had nothing to spend. But she did not want him to spend anything; she knew actors lived from hand-to-mouth. She wanted to buy him a painting as well: it would please her to, so he must not object. He liked to give pleasure, didn't he? Then he must not deny her hers. She did not mention the broken mirror: it must be cancelled out, the fracture atoned for. They went to a gallery and he chose a small oil, a landscape, by a nineteenth-century Scottish painter to add to his collection. He would put it on his wall where he could see it when he wakened in the morning. She felt caught in a flurry of desire for giving, she wanted to lavish gifts upon him. No more. He shook his head. They walked hand-in-hand, he carrying his presents under his arm.

They turned into a close and he put the parcels by his feet, propped them carefully against the wall. A delicious apprehension set her body tingling. Her laugh was cut off by his mouth. She put her arms up around the back of his neck, he put his around her waist beneath her coat. They stood there, like young lovers, she thought; she said. 'We are young lovers,' he said.

Lying in bed beside Farquhar that night, remembering how she had stood in the close with Conal, she was amazed at how oblivious to the passing world she had been. Any one of her neighbours' husbands or her husband's colleagues might have come by (it was not far from the law courts) and seen her in the arms of a man young enough to be her son. The bed shook with her laughter, and Farquhar snorted, half-wakening, and asked if she was having a nightmare. Go back to sleep, she told him; she was not upset. They had stayed in the shelter of the close for a long time, she leaning against the damp wall, he standing between her and the world, protecting her. He felt like a protector although on the surface he had few of the properties of one. He did not even have a room to take her to, not one where his mother would not be sewing in the other room, her feet flying on the treadle, her hands guiding the material. To be alone in a room with Conal? Would it be possible, and all that that would imply? Would he really want to make love to her? He had said that he would. She got up, unable to lie still. Farquhar was muttering again. She went to Camilla's bed and lay in the dark holding the teddy bear and thought about holding Conal. To give herself sexually to a new man at her age, a younger man, to have him look at her body, see the lines and folds of age? Her face burned. She was deceiving herself with thoughts of France and lying on the settee in front of the log fire. Naked on a settee, the size that she was? Conal said he loved her largeness: to him it meant abundance, generosity, peace. He could find peace inside her, he had said, as they stood in the close that afternoon. So many people seemed to be looking for peace; she too, she presumed, although she seemed to have had an abundance of it during the last few years, except for outbreaks of anxiety over Camilla. But perhaps peace did not describe the state she had inhabited: that was something more akin to the sensation of being adrift in a vacuum, which could only be described in negative terms. And peace was not negative. She wanted something positive now, vigorous, flowing; she no longer wanted to be caught in a sluggish backwater, a brackish pool hemmed in by stagnant undergrowth, watching the clear steady current flowing past. Body and mind: both were rebelling, struggling to break free, and would continue to no matter how much indignity or misinterpretation she might have to bear. There was a time when she thought the most important thing was to preserve one's dignity; not to lose face meant survival. But now she could not believe that appearances meant much at all, except to the onlookers. And she was done with onlookers.

Fine words, Emily Mountjoy! At least she could feel them; now she must see if she could hold to them. She smiled to herself as she fingered the worn fur of Camilla's teddy bear. She felt far from sleep. She rose and went downstairs. Louisa was sitting in the kitchen reading and drinking milk.

'Couldn't you sleep either?'

They sat on either side of the table and Emily had a glass of carrot juice since milk was both fattening and contained cholesterol. Louisa talked about Aberdeenshire's castles and fortified houses – a rich treasure trove – and upstairs Farquhar snored.

'Men do seem to sleep more than women,' said Louisa. 'Poor dears. Such a waste of precious living time.'

Emily thought of Conal. She could imagine him sleeping and was sure he would sleep soundly and long. In the mornings when they were in France she would rise early and go down the hill to the village to buy fresh bread and waken him only when the smell of coffee was percolating through the house.

'I must go north in the spring,' said Louisa.

'I shall go south.'

'To Corfu, with Farquhar?'

No, no, it was not what she had in mind, not at all. Louisa did not ask what it was exactly, but ruminated a moment pursing her lips over the rim of her milky glass and then she said,

'Mrs McCreedy is a very determined woman, you know, Emily.'

'She must let go of her son sometime, surely? I had to let go of mine.'

But Mrs McCreedy would hold on to Conal like grim death, said Louisa: he was all she had. She thought he would follow the pattern of the Irish bachelor who did not marry until after the death of his mother.

'But isn't that just the peasant Irish? Those living at the back-of-beyond, on small crofts where the son's labour is needed?'

'Mrs McCreedy's habitat has nothing to do with her mores. Besides, her apartment *is* the back-of-beyond.'

Emily was not interested in marriage, not for herself; even considering herself in a situation bereft of Farquhar, she would not contemplate entering in to the state of matrimony again. For more than thirty years her marriage had stood, whereas Louisa, with four broken ones behind her, was more likely to make another one, and indeed was young enough yet to have children, although the leanness of her body did not seem to suggest that was a serious possibility. But one never knew, said Emily, and often women as thin as pencils produced fat, red-cheeked babies. Louisa shuddered, feeling the tearing asunder of her flesh that that would involve, and to have her belly slip open and the child yanked out of her in that way did not appeal either. Maternity, not in its normally accepted sense, did not seem to be for her; she could use her protective and caring instincts on other people. She liked looking after people.

'Yes, you do, don't you?'

When Emily returned to Camilla's bed she slept peacefully and woke to find the sun filling the room with golden light and Louisa

116

standing in the doorway holding a tray of breakfast. It was ten o'clock.

'Good gracious!' Emily shot upward sending the teddy bear spinning to the ground. 'Farquhar's porridge!'

But it was all right for Louisa had given Farquhar his breakfast, and cooked both the porridge and kipper to perfection. 'At least I hope so.' She grinned, set the tray across Emily's knees and sat herself down on the edge of the bed. 'He said it was exactly to his liking. But then I know he is very good-mannered.' Emily was certain he had spoken the truth, since he was addicted to it, and his good manners would only have extended to the avoidance of telling a total falsehood. She said it was kind of Louisa to have done it at all, which Louisa denied. Emily leaned back against the pillows and enjoyed her breakfast. Below, the daily help could be heard vacuuming.

They were disturbed by the door opening and Camilla entering in a rush. She tended to enter rooms in a hurry, which was out of character with the way she lived the rest of her life.

'You're up early this morning, dear.'

'I wanted to talk to you.'

At once Louisa left, and Camilla took her place on the bed. 'What are you doing sleeping in here?' She lifted the teddy bear and rocked it absentmindedly. 'Have you and Father had a tiff or something?'

Camilla should have known better than to suggest that since her mother avoided such futile things. 'Oh yes, peace at any price!' Not true, but she would not argue. 'Have you eaten, dear? You look pale. Have a piece of toast?' Camilla was not hungry. Then she remembered to ask what her mother was doing in bed at this hour. Was she ill? She'd got a fright when the help said Mrs Mountjoy was still in bed.

'I feel absolutely grand, Camilla.' She poured herself some more coffee. Breakfast in bed was most enjoyable. In France, when she had fetched the bread and made the coffee, she might get back between the sheets so that they could breakfast in bed together. She and Conal in bed together? Flesh upon flesh, flesh in flesh?

'Mother, you're spilling the coffee!'

'So I am. How clumsy!' She mopped it up. It was nothing, a

mere splotch on the sheet. She smiled at her daughter who was biting her nails with an intensity that verged on ferocity. Did she take out the resentment she felt towards Carl on her nails? But she had bitten her nails all her life, and no attempts, either psychological or painting the nails with a pink repellent, had broken the habit. 'What was it you wanted to talk to me about, love?'

'Mother –' Camilla removed her fingers from her mouth and took a deep breath. 'Mother, were you in the High Street yesterday? In one of the closes off it?'

'I might have been. Why, dear?'

'Carl said –' She was unable to say what Carl had said. She tore the remains of a nail from her little finger, drawing blood. Emily winced. Her daughter looked up at her. 'He thought he saw you.' Her voice tailed off.

'I'm afraid I didn't see him, Camilla.'

'No, that was what he said.'

Chapter Nine

FARQUHAR was reading a book about Edinburgh in its Age of Reason. Emily made no comment. She seated herself by the window with her back turned to him. It was snowing heavily outside, unusually so for the city which lay close to the sea. The lawn was smooth, white and untrodden, the branches of the trees feathered, the air clear and hushed so that a blackbird's twittering sounded like a clarion call. There was no doubt that snow did make the world look beautiful, erasing ugliness, dirt, sores, smoothly and swiftly; but sun would lift the spirit even higher, the kind of sun that did not shift in and out of cloud but flooded a valley unceasingly with warm golden light. It was not likely to be snowing in the valley of the Lot at this moment, though one could be less and less sure of anything, even the weather, these days, but by the first day of April surely the sun could be counted on to appear for a few hours daily? When Farquhar had been shaving in the bathroom that morning getting ready for church, she had telephoned the woman in Cheshire and booked her house for the months of April and May, and tomorrow, weather permitting, she would go downtown and book the car ferry.

She had gone to church with Farquhar, in order not to worry him. Standing beside him in the pew singing hymns she had had an almost irresistible desire to laugh and had to bury her face in a handkerchief. Slightly hysterical no doubt, carried away by her delicious madness. Laughter bubbled up easily in her at the moment. If only they knew what she, Emily Mountjoy, pillar of the family and the church, such a nice woman, never a nasty word to say about anyone, always terribly obliging about doing the flowers and running the White Elephant stall, and so dependable, was planning! Farquhar broke stride in mid-song to give her a look of such bewilderment that she then had to resist the desire to put her arms around him and comfort him. But he would have bristled under her touch, even if they had been alone. For a long time he had not wanted to touch her, in bed or out, which suited her. They avoided one another's eyes whilst undressing. She supposed they had grown stale together after so many years: that was the easiest thing to suppose. And yet some people grew closer the longer they were together and when one died the other said it was like losing an arm. She could not imagine feeling amputation with the departure of Farquhar. Oh, she would miss him of course, but in the most trivial of ways! Winding the alarm clock . . . Into the centre of her thoughts Farquhar had broken, tugging at her sleeve indicating that the hymn was finished and everyone was seated but herself. Margo Jamieson-Brown had been smiling encouragingly from across the aisle.

'That a map you're looking at?' asked Farquhar now, looking over the top of his book.

He could see that it was, obviously; but he was only mildly curious and so his interest was easily turned aside by some remark about Mrs Seton fancying France for a change. She had not seen Mrs Seton for days, though had heard her on the telephone, and did not care if she never ever saw her again. Never ever. Ah, if that could be a possibility! But she had learned early on that one spoiled things by expecting too much from life. Tread softly, carefully, a little bit at a time, when what one wanted was important. She slid her finger down the red line from Cherbourg to Dinan, then switched to yellow – who wished to compete with the mad French on their *routes nationales*? – crossing the Loire above Chinon, where they might stop for coffee, then on to Chateauroux, Bergerac, Villeneuve-sur-Lot. They might have to stop overnight somewhere, in the Indre perhaps. No point in killing themselves by driving too hectically.

'Which part's she thinking of going to?'

'Who, dear?'

'Mildred Seton.'

'Oh, I really don't know. She didn't say.'

They must stop for an hour in Bergerac. A pretty town, and she could show him the castle and there was a delicious charcuterie in the main street.

'She's certainly a damned intelligent woman, no question of that.'

'Mildred Seton. I would hardly – '

He meant Louisa of course: she should have known. He and Louisa had been having long conversations about eighteenth-century life and letters, as well as fortified houses; she had re-awakened interests in him, which pleased Emily immensely. It was a relief to discuss matters at the table other than upset prices and closing dates. High noon was seldom mentioned nowadays, though Emily presumed he still had them, but quietly.

'I always told you she was intelligent, Farquhar.'

'She's interested in everything. Not just her own subject.'

She had them reading biographies of Frank Lloyd Wright and Corbusier and was planning a tour of Scottish architecture when the weather would let up. Farquhar had agreed to chauffeur, a development Emily regretted slightly since it precluded Conal from joining their trips, but her desire to see Farquhar happy triumphed and, besides, she and Conal would make many trips together in the spring. They might go to Albi, see the strange brick cathedral, visit the Toulouse Lautrec museum . . .

'Pity the snow's come on,' said Farquhar. 'We might have gone to Craigmillar this afternoon.' Being under the auspices of the Department of the Environment the castle was open to the public all year round, and not restricted to merely seasonal openings. The snow might let up later, said Emily, trying to calculate how many miles from Cherbourg to Villeneuve, estimating the inches with her finger. The snow did let up and Farquhar and Louisa set off to see Craigmillar Castle, where they could stand on the ramparts and survey the council housing estate below and Louisa could recall how within the walls Mary Queen of Scots had intrigued with Bothwell to bring about the murder of Darnley. Emily declined their invitation to join them on the grounds that Elspeth and Davina might call, it being Sunday afternoon. Their hardiness was a match for the coldest of Edinburgh days, but Emily's own did not feel up to coping with the exposed ramparts of Craigmillar Castle. She preferred her buildings with roofs, as well as furnished; that way her imagination could transport her back and she could imagine life as it had been lived in the sixteenth century. But raw walls, exposed sky, and wind whistling through every aperture – and there was never any shortage of those – only made her long to be back home. No doubt the failing was hers, she would freely admit that. All that such visits did for her was to make her feel that the sixteenth century must have been a truly terrible time to live in, certainly in Scotland, which had been much more barbaric than its neighbour south of the border. Elspeth and Davina talked about past centuries with such enthusiasm that it seemed they wished they had inhabited any other than the twentieth which they claimed to find barbaric. Emily had often amused herself imagining them using the lavatorial holes in the floor and watching through the slits in the ramparts for the coming of rampaging and ravaging hordes from enemy clans.

They arrived that afternoon wearing galoshes over their brogues and two cardigans buttoned across their chests. They regretted that they had missed the outing to Craigmillar; it was a castle they much admired.

'It was kind of Farquhar to take this American lady to visit it.'

'I rather think it was the other way round.'

Before Emily could serve tea Camilla arrived, wearing an old pair of Carl's corduroys tucked into Wellington boots. There was no saying who the Wellingtons belonged to. She left great footprints up the white path. Without being asked, surprisingly, she removed the boots in the front porch and padded into the drawing room in thick khaki socks darned with puce thread over the toes.

'Carl's mending,' she said, as she dropped into a chair and stuck both feet out across the silk Chinese rug. 'He won't let me mend them.'

'Men's lib,' said Emily, with a smile, lifting the teapot.

Elspeth and Davina found mention of Carl embarrassing; they knew that Camilla lived with him and that many young girls did live with their boyfriends nowadays, but they still found it a most difficult area and did not see why they should pretend otherwise. Neither did Emily, who had told them so after one particularly disagreeable occasion when Camilla had gone on about Carl's sleeping habits, something to do with which side of the bed he preferred. The girl had done it deliberately and afterwards her mother had told her to grow up and stop trying to shock. *Epater la bourgeoisie!* Camilla ought to realise that her aunts were far too easy game and that shocking them only pandered to baser instincts in herself. She was never going to bring them to a point of revolution. Or herself. But Emily had refrained from adding that.

'No cucumber sandwiches?' said Camilla.

'Try a piece of angel cake, Elspeth. Louisa made it. She's a splendid baker.'

'How useful!' said Camilla. 'She can feed your bodies as well as your minds.' Her dislike of Louisa had turned out to be vitriolic.

'Both must be sustained, Camilla,' said Davina.

'What do you feed your mind on, Aunt Davina? *The Lady*? Or the *Edinburgh Tatler*?'

'If you've come to be insulting, Camilla, I think it might be as well if you left,' said her mother.

'Sorry,' muttered Camilla.

'And if it comes to developing minds I daresay your Aunt Davina has read much more serious stuff than you have in the past few months.' They were well known for their reading of nineteenth-century novelists. The work of the twentieth century seldom touched their hands, except for the poetry of John Betjeman whom they thought a delightful man.

Camilla concentrated on her piece of cake. She was looking none too well, thought her mother, in spite of all those health foods she and Carl carted back by the sackful. She had taken to coming every day recently, often for no declared purpose.

Emily passed around the coffee walnut cake.

'Another of Louisa's creations?' said Camilla.

The telephone rang, and Emily answered it in the study.

'I'm missing you,' said Conal. 'How the hell do you expect me to live through a snowy Sunday without a sight of you?'

The door opened behind Emily.

'Shall I fill up the teapot?' asked Camilla.

'Please do, dear. And perhaps you could look after the aunts till your father comes in? I've been called away.'

'Called away?'

'A friend in need.'

It was all in confidence; she could not explain, which was nothing but the truth.

She picked Conal up outside the library on George IV Bridge. He was leaning over the parapet looking down in to the Cowgate when she pulled up. He wore a fur hat and looked as if he had stepped out of *Dr Zhivago*.

'Wouldn't mind playing Zhivago.' He slammed the car door. 'I rather like parts that have a bit of dash and style to them. As well as those which are fraught with suffering.'

They went to the Botanic Garden which glittered like a silver fairyland. Their breath sent out little puffs in front of them. A few birds had left spiky tracks across the velvety white expanses but human beings were rare upon the ground. They passed only one, a man who was feeding the birds.

The hothouses drew them. As soon as they opened the door of the palm house a different world enveloped them. Emily loosened her fur coat. Conal removed his hat. The air was still and moist and warm. Water dripped. From without they could hear the roar of the wind; inside they were cocooned by glass and warm air and greenery. And the smell! The scent of the tropics. A heavy, pungent, heady odour. One recognised it without having been anywhere tropical, said Emily, as she stood feet astride on the path gazing upward at the tall palms which soared in defiance of winter, their crowns pressing against the glass roof. There were palms from North Africa and India, South America and New Zealand, Malaya and Japan. She touched the mahogany brown bark of one from Lord Howe Island whose age it would be possible to calculate from its bands of green. She was thankful that people were not ringed around in such a manner. Conal said that he had always loved coming into the hothouses as a boy on bitter winter days and had scarcely been able to bear the moment of re-entering the cold world. 'We will delay it as long as possible today,' he murmured.

They walked hand-in-hand, moving languidly; they passed through the door into the second palm house. In the middle stood a giant tree a hundred and fifty years old, from Bermuda. One could dance round it like a maypole, suggested Emily. Instead of dancing, he kissed her. The heat of his lips and of the air encircling them made her feel giddy. He led her out to the covered, open-sided walkway where the wind rushed about their ankles and made them tumble headlong through the next swing door into the room of the orchids and cycads. Once more their steps slowed. The renewed warmth seemed like a blessing; they received it gratefully, knowing they would not relinquish it again too easily.

Amongst the orchids and palms they loitered, stopping to read the latin names, and kiss one another, to touch a flower in bloom and then each other. All seemed exotic, esoteric: the plants, the blooms, the heat, their bodies. All seemed intertwined, interwoven, connected. Now they came to a stop and stood for a long time very close, scarcely breathing, scarcely moving, eye to eye, mouth to mouth, lips barely touching. The steamy heat was hypnotic. They no longer inhabited the city of Edinburgh. They were in the jungles of New Guinea, Java, and Madagascar. They were everywhere and nowhere. Every now and then he spoke her name very softly. He wished that they could go to Java or Brazil; anywhere, as long as it was far, far away. They might go to France, she ventured, in a whisper. Let us go then, he said, smiling. But she meant it: to go to France *was* a possibility. He drew back a little and she trembled, wondering if she had asked too much. How could they go? he asked. She said that she knew a house in a valley where nightingales sang and sunflowers grew. He sighed. It sounded marvellous and he would love nothing better than to go there if only it were possible. But it was, she cried, shattering the silence of the glasshouse. He shook his head.

'Your mother?'

'I have no money, Emily.'

She laughed. That was of no importance! She had enough for both of them. He protested; she insisted. Would he go? Would he? She waited for his answer, listening to the slow drip of water behind them.

'Of course I will go, Emily. Do you think I could resist it?'

The shadows lengthened on the white lawns outside, the sky darkened, changing from blue to indigo with bands of turquoise and sand and pale lemon-yellow streaking the horizon. Each second the colours shifted and changed and then the sky was black as ink and the gardens outside were but a glimmer of light. Inside the hothouse it was dark.

He spread his coat on the path under the overhanging fronds of a palm. They lay down together. She stretched up her arms and her fingers touched the fringes of the fronds. Then she let her hands slip down to clasp his head. It was so easy for her to let him make love to her here amongst the cycads and strange exotic orchids. The plants kept watch over them, enclosed them, sent out aromas to sweeten the air about them. She felt no conflict, hesitation, shame. The darkness hid the flabbiness of her thighs and the broken veins that ran like networks down the lower part of her legs. She opened to receive him and he entered, like one who had been there before and was coming home. She gasped with relief. She fondled his head, cradled it, ran her fingers through his dark curls.

'I never want to come out of you.'

'You never need to.'

They saw a black figure pass the other side of the glass; they lay very still, until it had gone. The plants stood like dark giants above and about them, weird, but not frightening. Nothing in their refuge was frightening.

After years of starvation to lie with Conal was like being at a feast which brought with it a resurgence of appetite, a feeling of celebration, and of rebirth. When she had last felt such intoxication Conal would just be being born. She said so and he said that did not matter, not in any adverse way. He hoped that their moments of joy might have coincided. He presumed he must have felt some on being born. And what of his mother? Emily did not bring her name to come between them. Little could have come between them on that tropical afternoon.

Exhausted, satiated, they fell asleep in one another's arms.

She wakened with an agonising knot of cramp in her left leg and jerked upright, alarming him. 'It's all right, just cramp.' He took her leg between his hands and rubbed with fury until the pain went leaving an ecstasy created by its absence. She pulled him back to her.

Afterwards, she lay with her head on the damp rough path and laughed up at his dark shadowy outline. They would have to go soon. They couldn't spend the night in here.

'We might be shut in, Emily!' He said it gleefully, like a small boy hoping for an unexpected holiday, a fire in the school, the teacher taken ill. He jumped up to try the door. It *was* locked! The dark figure must have done it in passing. There was another door to the hothouse but it too was jammed. Locks could be forced. He hated such vandalism, but supposed that this was one occasion when it could be justified. She hovered watchfully, cautioning him to take care lest he cut himself. He took a stone and smashed the lock cutting the edge of his hand a little. She sucked the blood from it.

The snow had stopped falling but the brilliant world they stepped in to was ice-cold and the wind felt as if it blew straight from the Russian steppes. It stung their eyes, tore at their clothes. Heads bent, slithering in the new snow, they made for the Inverleith gate. That, too, was locked. The garden shut at sundown and the sun had long since gone down. The stars were out, spread in glorious patterns across the sky. Emily stood looking up at them with wonder. How much more majestic winter was than any other season! It brought one closer to the feeling of a divine power operating in the universe than did summer which drew one down to the earth. When summer came she would celebrate that too and rejoice in the contact of the earth. As she had so recently in the hothouse: in there it had been summer. She didn't seem to care if she was locked in or not, said Conal teasingly, as he eyed the spiked gate which was some six feet high. They could go back to their hothouse, she suggested, and spend the night there wrapped in her fur coat. That would be lovely, he said, but what about her husband? He would have the police out, again: they would find her car abandoned outside the gate and send in a search party.

'You are going to have to climb the gate, Emily, my love,' he said.

Chapter Ten

MRS MCCREEDY was restless. It was seldom that she paced floors –
there was little scope anyway for that activity in her flat – or
fiddled unnecessarily with things like fire tongs and hearth brushes.
But that Sunday afternoon she did sweep up the hearth when
there was no ash to collect on the little brass shovel, poke the fire
vigorously, get up and down to listen at the door for feet on the
stairs. One pair came up: it was the same woman again, the
one who drank. She was in a pathetic state and Mrs McCreedy
sighed but could not admit her, and said no, Conal was definitely
not at home.

He was definitely not in which of course was why she was restless. She even went to the window and stood looking down on the
market. She knew rather than saw what the scene was. Sundays
were quiet, dead quiet, but more so when falling snow kept
folk indoors in front of the television and trapped tourists in
sterile hotel lounges; few cars were parked, shops were padlocked
and grilled, and the down-and-outs were sheltering wherever they
could find overhead covering. No doubt there would be at least
one sheltering inside their stair door. Perhaps on such a day the
hostels relented and let them come in before the normal opening
time. It was not opening time yet for the pubs either, not till
half past six, but at least they could open now on the Sabbath and
that brought a slight flurry of activity. On Sundays she did not
have customers either, though often she sewed, but not with the
machine, doing hand sewing only, which was quiet and would
not disturb Conal. Most Sundays he liked to sit by the fire and
read or learn his lines or talk to her or play music on his hi-fi.
They had gone to church in the morning and that American girl
had sat behind them. Afterwards, she had joined them and they
had stood in a huddle, the wind swirling around their ankles and

Conal had seemed in no hurry to move. He had talked animatedly and snowflakes had drifted into his open mouth. Eventually, he had noticed his mother shivering and said they'd better be off.

He had been abstracted over lunch, did not even compliment her on her steak pie which was one of his favourites. He had got up and put on Schubert's Trout Quintet. 'It's vivacious, isn't it?' he said, and she had the feeling he was not speaking to her. He was thinking of another woman. There had been women in his life before, naturally; many of them, indeed most, having been her customers. It was how he had met them and she had never minded, except occasionally, but those moments of disquiet had usually passed. Of late he had been out a great deal, and often with those two women. When she made some remark about that opinionated American he turned on her quite fiercely, only to apologise quickly. But the memory of the fire in his eyes remained. She clenched her hands together, until she felt the nails dig into the back of her knuckles. She could hardly believe that he would be beguiled by that stick of a female whose chest was as flat as a scrubbing board and whose behind was like the rump of a stoat. Mother of God it was not possible that he would ever leave her for that! She went to the picture of the Virgin Mary and with eyes closed, head bent, said a prayer. She, too, had had a son, would surely understand and intercede.

It was darkening outside. He had said he was going for a walk, felt the need of some fresh air. He must come back soon. He would not walk in the dark and cold. She picked up a dress of blue velvet to hem the bottom but after two stiches laid it aside to go again to the front door. A blast of freezing air came up the stair to strike her in the face. Surely he could not be walking in that. He must be with *her* somewhere.

He *had* been with a woman. She smelt it on him as soon as he came in; she always could. It was very late when he did come and she had been as near to a point of panic as she had ever been in her life. Her relief made her reproach him, which, again, was unusual for her. But the day had not been usual. She had thought he might have had an accident! Doing what? he asked. Not much could happen to him on foot on the Sabbath. A car might have skidded and mounted the pavement, she had heard of such an accident on the news the day before.

'Where did you go, Conal?' she tried to ask the question lightly.

'The Botanic Garden.' Suddenly, he laughed, wholeheartedly and delightedly, as if he could not resist it, reminding her of his father whom she seldom remembered now, not in any emotional way. She might mention his name, repeat anecdotes, but that was not the same thing. She put her hand over her chest.

'It must have been shut hours ago.' Then she noticed the scuffed knees of his trousers and his bleeding hands. At once she ran for disinfectant and warm water and bathed his hands in the basin before the fire, although he protested and said she was fussing over nothing. And then he quietened, sat quite still and allowed her to administer to him, so that she would be soothed and afterwards they would be able to sit peacefully together and listen to some music.

The wind was wild that evening; hail whipped the window in violent flurries almost drowning the notes of Mozart. The fire roared up the chimney as if it wanted to escape. 'It's seemed a long winter,' said Mrs McCreedy, hands motionless at last for the day. They rested in her lap appearing strange by their very immobility. 'And there's still a lot to come. March can be the worst month.'

'Yes,' said Conal. He was staring into the leaping flames. She stared at him, hand on chest again. 'I was thinking – '

He was thinking of going away : he did not need to say any more. She often said they were telepathic. Oh, only for a holiday, he was quick to add, and she said, what else, he was not thinking of emigrating, was he? Emigration. The very word sent a chill down into her, ancestral perhaps, linking her back to starving people who had set sail in ships seeking a land of plenty. Many of her mother's ancestors had set off for North America, some had reached it, were settled now in places like Cincinatti and Pittsburg, and some had even come over to Britain seeking their ancestral roots. Once a woman with blue hair and blue-rimmed glasses had tracked her down and she had had to deny that her mother had been a Flynn from Monaghan and her grandmother's name was Cecilia. What did it matter? She felt no bond with the blue-haired woman standing on her doorstep. But what if her own next-of-kin was to go and live in Chicago?

'Are you short of money, Conal?'

He shrugged. She went to the Chinese vase on the mantelpiece but he got up quickly saying, 'No, I don't need anything, Mother. I've got that modelling job on Wednesday, for that wool firm.' She closed his lips tightly together. She did not like his face appearing on knitting patterns. He said that she was silly to mind: it was honest work and someone had to do it. They were using him to tempt the women, she said; to make them feel they might transform their husbands into images of him. 'Half of our lives are based on trying to imitate images,' he said. 'Not yours,' she said. 'You are yourself.' He seemed amused at that.

He got up to go to the window where he stood looking out into the dark violent night.

'You haven't seen Mrs Stewart recently? Were you not to phone her?'

'I've been too busy.'

'She's a nice woman is Mrs Stewart. I've a lot of time for her. She's always wanting me to go and visit her and see her house. She has a beautiful house, has she not?'

'Very beautiful. Like a picture in a magazine.' He picked up a book. She could not quite make out the title but thought that the word France was in it.

'Of course Mr Stewart was a very wealthy man.'

'Seems to have been.' He began to turn pages, look at pictures. He stopped at one, smiled at it. 'Villeneuve-sur-Lot,' he said softly, so softly that she could not distinguish the words.

'Emily, you know that we have no intention of going to the Lot this year.'

'It's quite all right, dear. I made the booking for a friend. I shall ring Cheshire in the morning and explain the confusion.' The woman had unfortunately rung back to confirm some small point whilst she was out and Farquhar had taken the call.

Which friend? Of course he had to ask that and she said some- one he did not know, a lady who worked in the charity shop beside her. Then he must know why the woman had not been able to make her own arrangements. His discipline demanded that he pursue a line to the point of its exhaustion, and hers.

'Oh, Farquhar, I'm tired!'

And no wonder! Imagine getting herself locked inside the Botanic Garden and having to climb the gate! He had never in all his life heard of such a ridiculous affair and intended to lodge a complaint. The attendants should make sure that the gardens were cleared before locking up. They usually did go round fairly thoroughly. Louisa interceded to say that perhaps the weather had made them make a more perfunctory check than usual. She smiled at Emily from behind her wide glasses. At least Emily had got out; otherwise she might have suffered a very cold night inside.

'You could have died from hypothermia,' said Farquhar.

'I could have gone back to the hothouses.'

'Wouldn't they be locked?'

Louisa thought perhaps Emily should go to bed; she offered to make her a hot toddy and bring it up. It was already settled that Emily would sleep in Camilla's room in case Farquhar in his sleep might kick her grazed knees.

Emily lifted her fur coat and held it up. 'I think I'll give it to Camilla for her shop. It does look somewhat the worse for wear, doesn't it?' she said cheerfully.

Louisa brought up the hot toddy and found Emily settled in bed.

'Are you sure your knees are all right? You don't think you should go to see the doctor tomorrow?'

The doctor would prescribe a tranquilliser or an antibiotic and she needed neither. She sipped the toddy. Louisa perched on the end of the bed, her bottom taking up very little room. Emily said she felt gratified to know that she had still been capable of climbing a six-foot gate at all. 'You look delighted,' said Louisa. 'At my age one doesn't expect to be able to do all sorts of things,' said Emily. 'We accept limitations too easily, don't we? At least I know I have. Perhaps you, Louisa, have not.' 'Oh, I don't know. We all limit ourselves one way or another. Sometimes it must be necessary, I guess.' Total indulgence would be disastrous? Could be, said Louisa. But she would not be the one to argue against it with any conviction. There might be something to be said for going to extremes at times; perhaps in that way one might find oneself.

Emily settled back against the pillows. Many parts of her ached but the pains were all pleasurable, even the stinging over her kneecaps where she had grazed them on the side of the stone gatepost. Pain and pleasure were so finely separated at times. She felt no temptation to confide in Louisa about her hours in the hothouse with Conal – even if she had considered it wise – for she never had been one to confide such intimate details to friends. To none of her friends had she spoken of her union with her West Indian. They had concluded what they wished from their own observations.

'Did you enjoy Craigmillar?'

Louisa enthused about the battlements. Farquhar had been most kind, had stood in the teeth of the icy wind whilst she photographed the building from every angle. From her father she had learned all about photographing buildings, and it could not be done in ten minutes. 'He's so fantastically patient,' she said, meaning Farquhar. Emily smiled, drained the last drop of the toddy. She felt very sleepy. Louisa said Farquhar was going to take her to Dirleton Castle tomorrow afternoon. He thought he could treat himself to a half-day as the market was quiet at the moment. 'Another ruin,' said Emily. 'You won't mind if I don't join you?' She could hear her voice getting fainter. Her eyelids drooped. Louisa was going to write to the owners of all privately owned fortified houses that were not open to the public and Farquhar had offered to write to a few with whom his firm had connections. 'Splendid,' murmured Emily on the way down. 'Simply – '

Louisa removed the glass from Emily's hand and turned out the light. Farquhar was still up when she went downstairs; he had some books open on his desk. A few things that might interest her. And would she care to join him in a little nightcap?

Carl was delighted with the fur coat. 'Sure you don't want some bread for it? I can easily sew up that rent.' Emily shook her head. Well, in that case she must have a look through the stock and choose anything she fancied. They had just got in a gorgeous

Japanese kimono in shades of turquoise and orange. Her interest perked up, She might well fancy that, if it were large enough. It would be, said Carl.

'What did you do with your coat anyway, Mother?' said Camilla, who had already asked the question.

'You wouldn't believe me if I told you so I shan't bother.'

Carl laughed. 'Come on, let's all go for a beer.'

Emily and Carl drank Guinness and Camilla ordered orange juice, rather pointedly, with a meaningful look at Carl, her mother thought. Was she pregnant? Surely not. Camilla had made a point of telling her when she went on the pill. She watched them over her drink. There was something wrong, they were quite out of tune with one another. Perhaps Carl had grown tired of Camilla. She felt a sudden wave of compassion for her daughter, wished she could gather her up into her arms as she had wished she could have done to Camilla's father yesterday, but knew she would receive the same response. Camilla had never liked to be cuddled as much as the boy, would push her away, slide off her knee. Like father like daughter, she presumed; or need it be that way? She must like to lie in Carl's arms. But then that was different. She longed to do something for Camilla but did not know what she could do. Any offer would be rejected, and she could sense the girl's hostility even now. Carl liked her and Camilla resented that. Well, that was understandable, especially since Carl did not love her as much as she wished.

'You look peaky, dear.' She could not resist saying it, in spite of knowing it would do less than good, but needed to let her mothering instinct find at least that small outlet. Habits did die hard. She went on to recommend a course of iron pills. Camilla sullenly said that she looked pale in the middle of every winter and who wouldn't, it had been so perishing cold?

'Your mother looks blooming,' said Carl, not helping at all. He did not care if he hurt or pleased Camilla, Emily realised, and longed to tell her daughter to leave the man, get up out of the basement and from under the bundles of old clothes and expose herself to light and air.

She took them for a wholefood lunch and then they went to the shop to look at the kimono. It fitted like a dream, said Carl.

Camilla said kimonos were not meant to fit, they covered any-body, and what exactly did a dream fit like? Every moment she was becoming more and more aggressive. Emily decided to re-lease them from her presence, to let them have their spat, or whatever it was they were building up to, and then afterwards he might make love to her on top of the bundle of old bedcovers and curtains and for a while at least Camilla might smile again. She had a lovely smile when she allowed it to come through.

'I'd love to have the kimono,' she said, taking it over her arm. She would wear it in the farmhouse, in the evening, when they sat in front of the fire. They were going to spend a lot of time sitting before the fire! It was always how she saw them, relaxed, his arm around her shoulders. All passion spent!

'What do you keep smiling about, Mother?'

'Nothing, dear. Just a little private joke. Must fly!'

Carl insisted on walking with her to the car. On impulse she said to him, 'I'm worried about Camilla. She doesn't look happy.' He frowned. 'I'm sorry, Emily.' She touched his hand, could say no more.

Since waking that morning she had wanted, and yet not wan-ted, to see Conal, not knowing how she would feel when she saw his face in the light. Since they had become lovers – and it was only in those terms she could think of it since she belonged to a certain generation – she had not seen his face. The scramble over the gate had been hectic, with him pushing her up from behind until at one point she had stood alone, queen of the castle, pre-cariously balanced, surveying the street. 'Keep down,' he had hissed and immediately, obediently, she had crouched lower and waited for him to come up behind her. 'What a lark, eh, Emmie? And don't start to laugh for Christ's sake! The gate's shaking. We don't want the fuzz on our tails. Wouldn't it look good – wife of eminent Edinburgh lawyer caught shinning over Botanic gate?' She told him not to say such things; it would only start her laughing. He leapt down from the gate first, landing lightly on the pavement below. He had done some ballet training at one point in his career, or non-career, as he called it. He held out his arms. 'Jump! And for God's sake mind the spikes.' She would have jumped from the top board of the Commonwealth swimming pool if he had commanded her. 'I have total faith in you, do you know that?' She shouldn't have, he said; it was too much for anyone to live up to. He caught her in his arms as she came down and the force of her weight sent them both reeling over backwards on the snowy ground. Now he laughed and it was she who had to hush him for she could see a car slowing and a man eyeing them with curiosity. From then on their progress homeward had been respectable.

She must go up now to the McCreedy's flat, could not stay away. She took the kimono with her as it would provide the excuse to call. It could do with a little letting out under the arms, if Mrs McCreedy would be so kind and was not too busy, and if she was, then no matter. The dressmaker had a client in who was about to leave. She invited Mrs Mountjoy in.

'Mrs Mountjoy, Mrs Stewart.'

The ladies inclined heads towards one another. Mrs Stewart was around her own age and looked and smelled expensive.

'I should have it ready a week today then, Mrs Stewart.'

'That will be fine.' She drew on honey-coloured suede gloves, smoothing out each finger. 'And you'll ask Conal if he'd like to come to that cocktail party with me? It'll just be five to seven, that kind of thing. We might have dinner afterwards.' Emily did not hear any more. The woman was saying something about restaurants, mentioning one or two that she knew Conal favoured.

'I'll get him to ring you,' said his mother.

Mrs Stewart nodded again to Mrs Mountjoy who did not return the salutation and was escorted out by Mrs McCreedy.

Why did all those horrible old clichés always come to mind at times of great pain? It was as if the brain could not cope with anything else. There's no fool like an old fool. The words ran through her head like a jingle; she seemed to hear them being chanted in the voice of Camilla.

'Well, Mrs Mountjoy, what can I do for you?' Mrs McCreedy, brisk, businesslike, was back. Emily told her why she'd come but added it was not important, she should really not have troubled her. The dressmaker did not mind being troubled, invited her to sit down and she would set the kimono to rights here and now.

Mrs Mountjoy tried to leave but Mrs McCreedy seemed determined to detain her.

The kimono was tried on and the dressmaker said a half-inch under the arms would make all the difference and would take but half an hour to sort. She should just wait whilst it was done. There was great determination in the woman, thought Emily, as she did as she was told and took Conal's chair. Mrs McCreedy sat down opposite and began to unpick the stitches.

'And how long is your young American friend planning to stay for, Mrs Mountjoy?'

Emily said she had no idea.

'She's living off you, is she?'

Emily said that she would not describe it as 'off', but she was staying with them.

'Your husband can't like that too much.'

Emily said he enjoyed her company, now.

Mrs McCreedy nodded her head over the kimono. Mrs Mountjoy should watch that; she was a sleekit one, that Yank, if ever she'd seen one. Emily watched the door, listened for sounds beyond the flat. In the adjoining apartment someone was listening to a racing commentary. She wanted to ask if Conal was due home but could not bring herself to speak his name.

The door opened abruptly and she thought she would faint. The old hot flush rose up from between her breasts to set her neck and face aflame.

'Conal!' cried his mother, rising. 'I didn't expect you yet.'

'I must go, Mrs McCreedy,' said Mrs Mountjoy. 'I'll come back . . .' She could not find her handbag which had got lodged beneath the seat. He recovered it for her. She did not look at his face. She left without looking at it.

She ran down the stairs, forgetting about taking care on worn steps, forgetting the pain in her knees. She did not slip. She felt sure-footed. He was calling after her but she did not stop.

She went out into the street and got into her car. As she drove off she saw him standing in the doorway of his stair. He did not move.

Louisa and Farquhar had had a most interesting visit to Dirleton, had lunched first at the inn there, and then spent a couple of hours going over the castle. Farquhar looked a little blue in the face but was cheerful. He and Louisa talked about the castle's history over pre-prandial evening drinks. Emily drank and did not speak.

When the telephone rang Farquhar went to answer it.

'Are you all right, Emily?' asked Louisa.

'I'm fine.'

'You didn't mind me going with Farquhar – '

'No, no – '

He came back to say the call was for Louisa. She left the room.

'You all right, Emily?'

'I'm fine, Farquhar, thank you.'

'You didn't mind me going out with Louisa, did you? You know there's nothing – '

The door opened and Louisa came in saying that her friend wished to have a word with Emily.

'Why did you run away, Emily?' asked Conal. There were many things she might have answered but said nothing. To admit again that she was jealous of another woman would be humiliating. Was she still there? He rattled the receiver, beginning to sound a little angry. She said she thought it would be better if they did not see one another again. She felt like a girl of seventeen. Now he was silent, then said in a tight voice, 'I see.' What did he see? He had to put another coin in the slot. She could hear passing cars and someone coughing. Could he see her at least once more to talk things over? To see him was the last thing that she wanted. Such a conversation was dreadful, she thought, as she circled her finger round the edge of the table on which the telephone stood. *Round and round the garden* . . . Such conversations went on all the time. 'Emily, do you regret yesterday? Is that what it is? What happened in the Botanic Garden?'

'No,' she cried. 'Not that!'

'Thank God! What the hell is it then?'

She told him.

'Mrs Stewart? But I have never made love to her in my life.'

'You're sure?'

'I swear it, for Christ's sake. I swear it standing here in the public telephone box beside the gents' lavatory, with a bloody gale blowing in through the broken panes.'

She had to commit Farquhar to Louisa's care for the evening. Louisa said that she did not mind, she would put the finishing touches to the meal, keep him happy. Farquhar said nothing, having ceased to make objections to her odd comings and goings.

Conal was waiting round the corner in Victoria Street sheltering in a shop doorway. She looked at his face and went forward to kiss him full on the lips.

'You are an idiot!'

They went to a small French restaurant in a cellar where they could sit close together in a corner, drink red wine, hold hands and talk. Eventually they could eat too, said Emily, thoughts of which reminded her of Mrs Stewart. Mrs Stewart was an old friend, said Conal; she must allow him to have friends. She was a wealthy widow who wished to remain one but sometimes she liked to be escorted to a function by a man who made no demands on her. So he acted as a kind of escort? She said the words uneasily. Did she find anything wrong with that? She supposed not, did not like to ask if he was paid for it or not. Amateur or professional? It was a bit like the question of his acting again. She felt muddled. He said gently that he could assure her that there was never any sexual involvement between him and Mrs Stewart, nor likely to be. 'I'd really have no right to object, Conal, even if there was.' Rights had nothing to do with feelings: he understood that. 'Anyway, Mrs Stewart's sexual tastes lie elsewhere. She is more likely to fancy you than me.' At once the knot of tension in her eased and she thought how foolish she had been to suffer so over the past few hours. It must be how Camilla suffered over Carl.

'At my age I should know better, Conal.'

'I wish you would stop saying, "at my age"!'

She apologised. He poured more wine, they raised their glasses.

'To orchids and cycads!'

They clinked glasses and drank.

'Unfortunately the hothouses will be closed by now. We shall have to find pastures new.'

'Conal!'

'Well, will we not?'

139

As long as the pastures were dark she would be happy and they were bound to be for this was not a town in which one might rent a hotel room for an hour, or at least not to her knowledge, and they could scarcely slip into her house or his room.

'Don't look now, Emmie, but there's a couple over there watching us.'

She had to look.

Margo Jamieson-Brown waved from across the room.

Chapter Eleven

EMILY MOUNTJOY was well aware that most of the people around her – her nearest and dearest, as their minister would designate them – were watching her with a certain amount of uneasiness, even apprehension. She could do nothing about it and comforted herself with the knowledge that for many years she had suffered uneasily over them, in varying ways. Responsibility had to stop somewhere.

Daily, Camilla visited the family home, from which she had been so keen to flee, often finding that her mother was absent. The cleaning woman said she didn't know what had got into Mrs Mountjoy these days, she was aye gadding about, didn't seem to be interested in the shine on her floors any more, so why should she wear herself out slaving her fingers to the bone working on them? The house was beginning to look neglected, even Camilla noted that: the skirting boards were gritty, dust lay undisturbed on the inlaid mahogany, and grease collected behind the cooker. Mrs Lamb blamed that American. Louisa was an easy target. Poor Louisa, thought Emily, but then Louisa could take care of herself extremely well and was unlikely to be perturbed by looks of censure cast at her by Mrs Lamb who was pointedly polite in a manner which was meant to be insulting. Louisa was not insulted. When Camilla did manage to cross her mother's path she guzzled continuously on her nails and gazed at her with her wide-open, beautiful eyes. There had been a long spell when Camilla had not looked her mother in the face at all. Sometimes Emily spent an hour or two with Camilla and Carl; she had taken the habit of dropping in on them, bringing a bottle of sparkling wine which they drank sitting on the old clothes. They laughed a lot, Emily and Carl.

Davina and Elspeth had been confided in to some extent by

their brother. They were sympathetic, or strove to be, knowing it was a difficult time for a woman. They themselves had been through it but had bothered no one, except each other, had not even gone to the family doctor for they did find it embarrassing to talk of such matters with him. They had known him most of their lives, went to dinner with him and his wife. They invited Emily to tea but she seemed to be busy, kept promising to come and never did. It was that American woman of course who was using her, as she was using Farquhar also. They tried to say so to him but he brushed their cautionings aside saying that they had a huge empty house and what was wrong with letting a stranger have the use of one room? It scarcely seemed Christian to turn people out into the streets. After that they were a trifle cool with him, feeling that he had called their sincerity as Christians into question. They withdrew a little, decided not to give dinner parties except for special occasions; it was becoming impossible to have their brother and his wife whom they usually did include, since her behaviour was so unpredictable and even he had changed in some way which they could not quite put their fingers on. They talked about it over their evening beverage, puzzling, sighing, feeling the break-up of their civilisation. They were glad they were not young in this era.

The Jamieson-Browns also decided it would be best to exclude the Mountjoys from their dinner list for a while. They were discreet, had mentioned to no one what they had seen in the French cellar, although Douglas had asked Farquhar casually over a round of golf if Emily was all right these days, saying that Margo felt a bit worried about her, thought they were growing apart. Farquhar was non-committal; he swung his club, and the matter was dropped.

Farquhar himself was trying not to watch Emily. He was not sure what she was up to and did not wish to find out. Restraint came easily to him; there was no difficulty involved in being unable to pry. No doubt all this would pass, the craze for Yoga, rushing around the city, visits to the theatre and God knows what else. In the meantime, when he was not working, he took Louisa on excursions around the countryside to see buildings of historic or architectural interest – outings he enjoyed immensely – and he read more widely than he had done for years. One got into a rut so easily, he confided to Jamieson-Brown, as they walked between holes, one had always meant to read and do so many things and suddenly one found life was going past too quickly and the daily round seemed rather banal. Now Jamieson-Brown glanced at him uneasily. He confided later to Margo that he was a bit worried about Farquhar; he seemed to be not quite himself. Margo made a remark about the male menopause which was not pursued. Douglas's own change of life crisis had been accompanied by an affair with a younger woman, but it had not been serious, or so he had always said. Since then things had been fine between them though, as she had told Emily, she had never been able to trust him totally again. She could not take unfaithfulness lightly, as some did nowadays.

As for Louisa: she watched Emily openly and knew what she was up to, more or less, though did not know about the French trip. About that Emily was most careful, keeping all the papers relating to it in a locked box under Camilla's bed where she continued to sleep. She and Louisa talked obliquely about herself and Conal. He might be a womaniser, suggested Louisa. Emily knew he liked women more than men and at one time would have tended to condemn a man for that, but why should she? Louisa was surely not going to give her lectures on the desirability of being all-rounded and well balanced? 'Hardly.' Louisa laughed. She was troubled though, hoped Emily would not be hurt, an anxiety she did voice, and added, 'Oh well, and what if you do get hurt once in a while?' She did, however, watch Conal also.

She found that she, too, was drawn to the McCreedy flat and would go as often as she could find an excuse. She circled the room as if expecting to find some clue, some key. She quizzed Mrs McCreedy about her life, and Conal's. Strange that he had never married. Had he never wanted to, been engaged? She could see that the dressmaker thought it was none of her business but did not mind that. Not everyone needed to get married, said Mrs McCreedy, jabbing a pin into the side of Louisa's half-made dress; it did not seem to do some folk much good. And she wouldn't exclude herself from that.

'Oh, I agree, Mrs McCreedy. It didn't seem to benefit me much either. But we can't be sure though, can we? I mean, it might have helped develop us as individuals. Just think if one had had no experiences, remained untouched, unmarked. Purity is of no particular advantage, except to the saints. And sainthood is hardly appealing to us ordinary mortals.'

'Conal is not aspiring to be a saint just because he isn't married!'

Louisa giggled. Not a becoming sound for a woman, thought Mrs McCreedy, as she lifted the hem of the garment and pulled it over her customer's head without taking her usual care not to snag the skin. She would not have minded if the pins had ripped the skin to bits. As she tugged the dress off, Louisa's hand came out and knocked her glasses off.

'Oh, Mrs McCreedy! Again! How clumsy I am.'

This time she put the spectacles back into their owner's hand at once. Mrs McCreedy settled them firmly over her nose. She saw the American woman's face coming back into focus, sharpening from a swimming blur into a pointed chin, thin nose, large steel-framed glasses covering eyes too big for the face. For a second they stared at one another. And then Louisa moved, to go to the window, her favourite place in the room.

'I'm sure Conal is no saint,' she said. 'He is too handsome a man for that.'

Without asking, she pushed up the window, and leant out. The dressmaker seized her fluttering paper patterns.

'You'll get your death if you hang out of there like that with nothing on.'

The American pulled in her bottom and closed the window. She was smiling when she turned round. She was hardy, she said, could withstand a lot.

'I do so love your little nest, Mrs McCreedy. I quite envy you, you know. This is your centre, and you are centred here.'

Mrs McCreedy continued to smooth her paper patterns, running her nimble fingers out to the very edges. She saw beneath the bottom rim of her spectacles a blur of movement, the white thin legs of Louisa gliding around her room. The invader. The enemy. Now the long white shapes had come to rest by the back wall. She was looking at the large portrait of Conal playing Hamlet.

'A lot of women must have been in love with Conal?'

'Yes, a great many.' His mother relaxed, for now she could speak the truth and have nothing to reproach herself for, no sin to confess. She patted the apricot-velvet chair. 'Come and sit yourself down, Miss Grant, and warm yourself by the fire.'

Emily and Conal were sitting on a seat in the National Gallery staring at Raphael's painting of the 'Holy Family with a Palm Tree'. The gallery was a good place for them to sit together, and this room was quieter than some others, since, being at the back, not so many people circulated. Emily's friends and acquaintances were unlikely to be amongst those circulating; they might go to the opening of an exhibition or visit the Louvre when in Paris but never think to turn into this gallery in the middle of their own city. Emily did not regard secrecy as essential but considered it better to keep themselves as private as possible. It was a difficult thing to do in a city where one had spent a lifetime, and where friends and acquaintances formed chains that linked and crossed and criss-crossed so that no area was free of potentially interested observers, unless one travelled out to the edges of wasteland. She knew no one who lived in a high-rise block, apart from her cleaning woman.

'When we're in France we'll be able to go where we choose as openly as we choose.'

'And do whatever we choose,' he added.

He smiled, shifting his gaze from Mary's face to hers for a moment. He had said that he wanted to make love to her in the open air, in the middle of a field, beneath the branches of a tree (one other than a palm, though he would not mind repeating that experience again either), beside a running stream. She had tried to tell him that she was less sure about that, she was a very private person when it came to private acts, but he had laughed away her apprehensions and said he knew her too well to believe that. She was capable of great abandonment, which was one of the things he liked about her.

They leaned back, hands clasped between them on the bench, and looked at the holy family. Emily felt slightly uncomfortable to see before her a palm tree in such close association with holiness, but Conal said it did not bother him in the least. As far as he was concerned holiness and happiness went well together. They were surrounded by madonnas with child. Nine in all. She had counted them and studied each face: the mothers', not the childs'. They ranged from the pert to the pensive, but all looked in possession of a secret. On their way through the gallery they had paused briefly in front of Rubens' 'The Feast of Herod' and Conal had said he admired the women of Rubens. She had tugged him on, hating the sight of the severed head and not wishing to dwell either on the fleshy contours of the women which both disturbed and reassured her. She was not as pinkly blooming as they, she told him, and he must accept that fact before he saw her fully in the flesh, but he would not listen. 'Silly Emily!' Was she exaggerating the ugliness of her flesh? At night, lying on Camilla's bed, she asked herself the question and could not find a satisfactory answer. Sometimes she had even got up and stood naked in the middle of the night to examine herself in front of the mirror, had winced at her large buttocks and heavy thighs and sagging stomach. Conal was so trim, so youthful. 'I like you as you are,' he said, not knowing what that was. 'Don't change a thing for me...'

She had brought pictures of the house in the Lot to show him, coloured snaps taken some years ago by Farquhar. She had removed the ones which included people. The house was L-shaped, whitewashed, with a clay-pink pantiled roof. Wisteria climbed the wall around the doors and windows. The blue-grey shutters were flung back against the white walls. Sun poured into the rooms beyond warming the wooden floors. Outside on the patio was a round table with a coloured umbrella and plates bearing bread and cheese and on the ground stood a bottle of red wine. It was all so typical, so obvious, but what one wanted, one sought out; here in this northern country they could not get enough sunshine or eating out of doors or flinging back of shutters. Here, one withdrew, closed the shutters of one's soul; there, one opened up, relaxed, received.

'It will all be marvellous,' he said, even if the spring sun would not be strong enough for them to sit outside, or lie on the ground, for inside they could build the fire and close the door.

'I wish we were there now. Let's go tomorrow, Conal!' she cried.

But tomorrow he opened in O'Casey. Of course she had not meant it, though it would have been nice if it were possible. She knew he could not let people down, fellow actors, producer, stage manager, front-of-house, ticket sellers, supporters of the club; and, also, his mother needed to be prepared. He was already working on that though and she accepted that he intended taking a holiday. He took one every year. He could not tell her with whom he was going : that would be too much for her to accept. He must say as little as possible, Emily advised; they must lay their plans, be patient, and in the end rewarded. With a bit of luck, she added, not depressed by admitting to the need for it. At the moment it seemed to be running with them strongly.

Conal opened in *The Plough and the Stars*. Emily and Louisa were in the audience, which was sparse. The size of the audience did not interest Emily who sat back entranced by Conal's performance. His sensitivity and understanding never ceased to delight and amaze her. His range was enormous.

'Don't you think so?' she asked Louisa at the interval.

'You must know more about that than me, Emily. Sorry, I didn't mean that to be catty.'

'I did not take it as such.'

'You have such great good nature, Emmie, that it worries me you could be taken for a ride.'

'You mean robbed and left bleeding by the wayside?'

'Perhaps, yes.'

'I don't have much money, Louisa. Not really.'

'You could raise a thousand or two.'

'If I wished. But I doubt if I intend to.'

The lights dimmed.

'You surely don't think he is after my money?' Emily chortled.

'Shush,' said someone behind.

'But, Louisa,' began Emily.

They were shushed again, must wait for the final curtain to finish the conversation, and as soon as the clapping died away Louisa returned to it as if the intervening break had not occurred.

'Do you know how he supports himself, Emily?'

She did not care very much, knew it was from odds and ends

and, all right, his mother's sewing, which she admitted was not admirable, but then we all did unadmirable things much of the time, didn't we? He was an artist, had integrity, could not cope with the commercial world.

'He is more commercial than you or I.'

'No!'

They were the only two people left in the auditorium. The girl in charge of front-of-house signalled to them from the back. They were trying to get cleared up.

Louisa and Emily moved outside.

'He's a gigolo.'

'Don't be ridiculous, Louisa!'

Well, maybe that was too strong a word, and too melodramatic, but he did get money from women from time to time, for services rendered.

'Are you serious, Louisa?'

'Oh hell! I didn't mean to tell you, not like that, not like this.'

'Let's go home,' said Emily.

Farquhar was at a legal dinner, the house was empty. The grandfather clock ticked distinctly in the hall. Emily opened the glass and silenced the hands. They went into the drawing room and sat down with a bottle of Farquhar's cognac.

'Now tell me!'

Louisa repeated what she had learned from Mrs McCreedy that afternoon. She was apologetic, distressed, full of hesitation, but Emily pushed her relentlessly on, wishing to know the truth. Perhaps not the whole truth for who could know that, not even Conal's mother, but an approximation must be known. When Louisa had finished they sat in silence.

It was only after a few minutes that they registered the ringing of the telephone. Emily went to answer it.

'Why didn't you wait for me, Em?'

'Come here and I will tell you.'

'You are mad,' said Louisa, whilst they waited for him to arrive. She looked ill. 'Farquhar may come back first.'

Then she could sidetrack him, entertain him, seduce him, do what she wished. Emily drank more brandy, paced up and down the velvet-piled carpet her body braced with energy.

Conal arrived in a taxi. Louisa brought him into the drawing room and then withdrew to hover in the hallway on the watch for Farquhar.

Emily gave Conal a drink, seated him on the settee, but would not sit herself.

'What is it, Emily? What in God's name has happened?'

She repeated the conversation she had had with Louisa. He refilled his glass himself taking a generous portion.

'Now tell me the truth! Is it true? Is any of it true?'

For a moment he would not lift his head. When he did he looked weary. She wanted to comfort him, to nurse his head. But she did not move, stood ramrod-still, as if encased in a corset like the one her mother used to wear and once had tried to get her to wear. Support the figure, girl, she used to say, and then you will never sag. Perhaps one should listen to one's mother more.

'Yes, some of it is true.'

'I see.' She was beginning to see. All those women . . . Now she did sit down, but in a chair away from him, so that a space separated them and he would not be able to reach out and touch her.

'But I'm not a bloody gigolo hiring myself out for sex.'

'You have taken money from women though?'

'They have given me presents.'

'Don't duck the issue!'

'I have never asked for anything.'

'But they have given you money in return for – '

She heard a car turning into the driveway. Farquhar back from his dinner.

'I've told you about Mrs Stewart.'

But there were others. Mrs Allan and Mrs Anderson and Mrs MacDuff . . . Quite a roll-call.

'God, my mother has been shooting her mouth off!'

The front door opened and Louisa's voice reached them. Footsteps disappeared into some other region of the house.

'Emily, you're married, you've slept with another man, he's kept you – '

'Kept me?' she cried.

He apologised. He had chosen the wrong word; he who was so

usually fluent was stumbling and fumbling for the right words now. But what he was trying to say was this: people did things for one another, life was made up of giving and taking, or should be, the shades of morality separating ways of life were often fine, and who was to make the judgment? The priest? she suggested tartly. She felt tart but not soured, not yet, although she knew that that might come later. 'You've been a good wife to Farquhar, pleased him – ' She interrupted. 'I doubt if I have ever pleased Farquhar.' Conal was silent, allowing her to add, 'Well, not that he would ever admit it anyway. Pleasure has not been too big a feature of our life whereas yours – ' His had been full of it: that he confessed to. He liked to please, to see gratification and enjoyment on the recipient's face; he thought always of the other person's enjoyment more than his own, whether in the theatre or in bed, though his own enjoyment, he hoped, must be a part of theirs, deepening and enhancing it. 'I've been honest, Emmie, and scrupulous, believe me! I've never offered or promised anything I knew I couldn't fulfil. I've always known my limitations and asked for no quarter where none was deserved, expected nothing for nothing. I've tried to retain my integrity. I've never acted in a play I didn't believe in or made love to a woman I didn't desire or at least wish to please.'

'And which – ?'

'I desired *and* wished to please you.' He made to get up. 'What more – ?'

No, stay back, she said, he must not come near her. Her voice trembled a little, devoid now of tartness to strengthen it. She could not cope with the close presence of his body: it seemed to melt her will as well as her limbs and cloud her head like an intoxicant.

'Conal, you must tell me – have you *ever* had sex for money?' She asked the question bluntly and felt blunted by knowing what the answer would be.

'I've been given presents – '

'Be honest now!'

'Very well, if you wish. Sometimes a woman has given me some money.'

She released her breath.

'I'm sorry you don't like it. It's the idea of the money, isn't it, that upsets you, more than the present of some object? But I repeat – I have never *asked* for anything.'

'But you accepted.'

'You see me now as an immoral man?'

'I don't know,' she said helplessly. She felt helpless to make a judgment : her standards had gone awry, she had no guidelines to keep her straight.

'I try not to hurt people, although sometimes I accept that I must.' He could say that his life had been based on giving pleasure, but surely there were worse things one could base one's life on? Most people based theirs on making money, often giving nothing to no one but themselves; some went out to destroy and kill, legally or illegally, whilst others were parasitical on their fellows or the state. She could now say he was parasitical, could she?

Oh no, he had earned his supper.

'Don't be bitter, Emily, please !'

A tap on the door announced Louisa. She poked her head round it. 'Just wanted to let you know that Farquhar is taking me for a drive. He's such a pet. I said I wanted to see Dirleton Castle by moonlight.'

Emily thanked her.

Louisa and Farquhar drove off to Dirleton.

'You've enjoyed the women though, Conal?'

He could not pretend otherwise. And if it was a crime then he pleaded guilty. 'Would you prefer that I had suffered? Emily, I've enjoyed you. I do enjoy you. I love you. But you're going to say you don't believe it, that I am saying it only to get round you . . .'

And he did get round her. They lay on the settee together and she reached out to extinguish the standard lamp. 'Don't do that,' he said. 'I want to see you, to watch your face.' But Farquhar and Louisa might return, she countered, stroking his head, allowing him to repeat his protestations of love, allowing him to tell her that it had never been like this with any of the other women. They had been bored with their husbands, had wanted a little excitement, an intrigue without danger, had gone into his room with him for a half-hour or so after they had come for a fitting, no more than that. That was the extent of his associations with them and they would have been terrified if the relationship had expanded into anything else. They did not want the balance of their lives threatened. They did not want him entering their drawing rooms, putting them at risk. Now she wanted to know all about the women, who they were, what they looked like, if they were fat or thin.

'There's one woman I've seen, one who drinks.'

Conal sighed. She was different, not because their relationship had been, but because she had been an unhappy woman and had wanted more from him than he could give. 'Sometimes that happens.' 'Yes,' said Emily, thinking of Camilla and Carl. Conal had had to tell the woman to stay away. She had left her husband, taken to drink, but would have done that anyway, and he did not believe he said that merely to absolve his conscience.

'Forget her now,' said Emily.

Forget them all, even Louisa and Farquhar who were walking in the moonlight chill in the village of Dirleton gazing at the dark outline of the ruined castle. It was one of those nights in which one could believe in ravaging hordes and impending danger, said Louisa, shivering; one could feel oneself transported back in time, to the last two years of the thirteenth century when the castle had first been besieged, by Edward I. Farquhar hesitated for a moment, whilst buttoning the cuff of his pigskin gloves, then he turned and put his arm around her, to shelter her from the wind. 'Edward I was nicknamed Longshanks. Did you know that, Louisa?' She laughed with pleasure, but whether it was out of amusement at Edward's nickname, or delight at the sight of the moon rising above the tower of the castle, or because she liked the protection of his arm about her, he could not tell.

Chapter Twelve

MARCH came in as gentle as a lamb, and therefore might go out as wild as a lion, as Emily told Louisa who had not heard of the saying. In the mid-west of America the month would not mean the same thing at all. In France, especially towards the south, things should be further forward, said Emily. 'Things?' asked Louisa. 'The trees, nature.' Emily became vague, as she did at times when she started to think aloud and then suddenly realised that she had. She was frequently preoccupied. The help had given notice; she did not like it when you talked to someone and she wasn't even listening. Previously, over cups of morning tea, Mrs Mountjoy had been most sympathetic. Mr Mountjoy thought they should get someone else but when he mentioned it his wife became vague again saying how difficult it was to get someone reliable, that you could leave, trust to do the work, not steal the silver; it was hardly worth the bother and she had always hated employing anyone to do anything for her. The silver had already been stolen, her husband reminded her drily, but she was no longer listening; her mind was running in channels where he could not follow. He was not over-fussy, he explained to Louisa, but rings of grime around the bath and fluff under the bed that made one sneeze did seem a bit much to put up with. The seeds of decay set in quickly, were soon sprouting in all directions, and before one knew it a property could deteriorate rapidly. He had seen it all too often in his line of business. Louisa began to vacuum under the beds and scour the bath and the cooker. Emily remonstrated with her but Louisa did not mind; it was a way of paying rent.

'I don't know what we should do without Louisa,' said Farquhar Mountjoy to his wife, as they set off for church on a Sunday morning, almost the only activity which they did together alone now

'Indeed neither do I, Farquhar. She's a delightful girl. I'm most fond of her, and she's great company for me.'

He cleared his throat. 'Emily, I was thinking that at Easter, when the season opens, I might take Louisa up to Aberdeenshire for a few days to see the castles. There are such splendid ones, Craigievar, Crathes – '

'What a marvellous idea!'

They turned in through the church gates and scrunched their way up the gravel. A few crocuses were poking their heads through the grass along the verges. The crocuses were flowering in the Botanics too; they had stopped to admire them yesterday, she and Conal, had seen them as signs not only of spring but of their new life together.

She was perfectly welcome to come with them, Farquhar was saying; but if she did not want to, there would be nothing for her to worry about, she could rest assured on that score.

'Worried, Farquhar? Why should I be worried?'

They entered the church; soft music met them, and an elder in a navy-blue suit holding out a hymn book. They sat in the pew behind the Jamieson-Browns. Margo turned to give them a little smile. Emily did not mind the service; she could sit in peace and think of south-west France, envisage them in the market, in the *routier* café at Sainte Livrade eating a six-course meal at a price which was an absolute steal. She knew she daydreamed a lot these days, let her thoughts drift off whenever the present became too dull to hold her. Throughout the hymns and prayers and sermon she smiled serenely, and Margo Jamieson-Brown, taking a quick glance backward, thought that Emily looked too untroubled to be up to anything seriously wrong. That incident in the cellar must have been due to some momentary aberration. Had Douglas not been with her she could now believe she had imagined it.

After the service the two couples turned to talk and when Emily suggested a pre-lunch drink at their place – it was ages since they had seen one another properly – the Jamieson-Browns accepted at once.

Louisa swooped into the hallway to meet them and Emily sensed that there was some complication to be coped with. She suggested Farquhar take their guests to the drawing room whilst she and Louisa looked for a few nuts and biscuits in the kitchen.

She closed the kitchen door behind them.

'Conal is in my room. I brought him back from church with me. He wanted to talk to you.'

Emily began to laugh. These moments of farce appealed to some previously submerged quirk in the make-up of her humour.

'He's a bit het up.'

Emily sobered, and went at once to Louisa's room, leaving Louisa to go and help entertain the Jamieson-Browns who were a little put out by Emily's absence. They sat side by side on the Regency-style settee sipping martinis and listening to a run-down on Aberdeenshire castles; and from time to time Margo glanced towards the door anticipating the entry of Emily who never came. What astounded them was Farquhar's seeming disinterest in the non-appearance of his wife and his incredible enthusiasm for castles.

After half an hour Margo excused herself. She went upstairs and used the lavatory since she did not wish to be dishonest but before returning downstairs toured the top landing pausing outside each door in turn to listen. From behind one she heard the voices of Emily Mountjoy and a man, and did not like what she heard. Swiftly she ran back down the stairs, stopping at the bottom to take a deep breath, holding on to the newel post. She felt most upset. She didn't count herself a prude, was doing her best to change with the changes in society, but if everyone abandoned their standards where would they end up? Nothing would remain sacred. And some things must. 'Some things must,' she said aloud.

'Are you all right?'

She looked up. Camilla was standing in the porch pulling off a pair of Wellingtons.

'I'm fine, dear. And how are you?'

Camilla, in stockinged feet, accompanied her to the drawing room, and at once Margo said that they simply must go, she had left a roast in the oven and they didn't want to eat charred roast beef, did they? She heard her laugh ring out hollowly: she felt the hollow. She wondered if she would ever again enter this house.

She had always been fond of Emily, would have staked anything on her sincerity and integrity. How could she have been so wrong about her? Or how could Emily have changed so much? She put her hand to her head, feeling a migraine coming on. For Emily to bring that man into her own house and take him upstairs whilst they were guests in her house seemed like obscenity for its own sake, a deliberate flouting of all their standards.

Upstairs, whilst the Jamieson-Browns were departing, Emily was telling Conal that he too must go. If he left by the back door and slipped through the garage no one would be any the wiser, except for Louisa. He had indeed been upset when she came up to him. His mother was unwell, had a pain in the left side of her stomach, and was going to the Infirmary on the following day for investigation. It was so unlike her, he kept repeating; he could not remember when she had last visited a doctor. Most pains turned out to be caused by less than organic causes, said Emily; she was a great believer in the idea that much of illness originated in the mind. But Conal did not like the way his mother was talking. 'Almost as if she expected the illness to be fatal?' He nodded. He must not worry, Emily said, adding a few platitudes about the worst never happening and so forth. She stroked his hair gently, touched his cheek, kissed him. He must go to see the doctor himself, once the results of the test were known; she insisted that he did.

Conal missed the Jamieson-Browns by about half a minute but ran into Farquhar as he was coming back from seeing them into their car.

For a moment the two men stood still, and then Farquhar's instincts caused him to react. 'Can I help you?' he asked. 'Were you looking for someone?'

Conal, wedged between Emily's car and her husband's Rover, said that he was looking for a friend, a Miss Grant. So Farquhar invited him in, and Louisa introduced him to Mrs Mountjoy and her daughter.

'May I offer you a drink?' said Mr Mountjoy.

'Please do have one, Mr McCreedy!' cried Mrs Mountjoy whom her husband and daughter observed to be in great high spirits. Farquhar wondered again if Emily could be taking drugs but Louisa had assured him that he should not worry on that account.

Conal stayed for an hour. It took Farquhar only five minutes to find out what he was, and did. 'Ah, an actor? That can't be an easy life, eh?' Camilla squatted on the floor cross-legged and gloomily studied her feet whilst over her head her father and the actor conversed about the current state of the theatre and Arts Council subsidies and on the other side of the room her mother sat with the American woman talking like conspirators on a level in which no words could be distinguished. They seemed highly amused and pleased with themselves. Every time Camilla came home now she felt that something odd was going on. Or was it her? Carl said at times when they rowed that she had distorted vision, saw everything and everybody through her own expectations, which was akin to looking through the wrong end of a telescope. If anything didn't work out the way she wanted she blamed other people. She was confused, did not know what to think, had come today to ask her mother, but looking at her now wondered if that would be possible; she no longer disapproved when formerly she always had, made no more remarks about the state of squalor in their flat, did not nag about fresh air and getting enough protein. Her mother was giving up her role, said Carl, and that was why Camilla was so disturbed. But why should she continue playing mother when her children had rejected her? She had not rejected her mother, Camilla had retorted sharply; he always exaggerated. She might say that to him for his mother lived in the south of England and he only went to see her once a year. They ended up having a row about their mothers which was quite ridiculous. They could have rows about anything these days, and when that point was reached there was only one solution, said Carl. Even under the circumstances? asked Camilla. Maybe especially because of the circumstances, said Carl. She told him he was a hard-hearted fucking bastard, but should have known that hard words would not move him.

'You'll stay to lunch, dear?' Her mother was speaking to her. 'And you, Mr McCreedy? Would you care to join us?'

He was sorry, said he would love to, but must go as his mother would be expecting him.

157

'Do you live at home?' asked Camilla.

'Yes.'

'How odd.'

He smiled and her mother reprovingly said, 'Camilla!'

'Well, I mean at your age . . .'

'My mother is a widow.'

'Suppose he's a pouf,' said Camilla, as her father carved the overdone roast beef. He raised the carving knife and frowned at her.

'Why do you say that, dear?' asked her mother.

'Any man over thirty who lives with his mother is bound to be.'

'One can never generalise, Camilla,' said Louisa, passing round the overdone yellow Brussels sprouts. 'That way one makes great mistakes.'

'She's ghastly, that female,' said Camilla, when afterwards she helped her mother with the dishes. Her father and Louisa had gone to visit Lauriston Castle. 'She talks as if she knows everything.'

'She's often worth listening to.'

'Aren't you worried she might be trying to seduce Father? No, I guess not. She'd have a hell of a job. Can you imagine? Father being raped against the battlements?'

'There are no battlements at Lauriston,' said Emily Mountjoy.

Conal returned home to find that his mother had kept his lunch warming in the oven. It was dried up, she was afraid. She shook her head sorrowfully. He did not mind but of course she did. Was she not eating? No, she had no appetite. She sat down to watch him eat, hand held against her ribs. Was she in great pain? he asked between bites, wishing he could slide the plateful of food into the flames but knew he must eat every scrap or offend her further. She could not cope with rejection of her food.

'Not in great pain.'

'It's probably just indigestion.' Or muscular, he added hastily, for to suggest indigestion bordered on frivolity, and there was no element of frivolousness in the look on his mother's face.

'Conal, whatever happens you must go on your holiday.'

What did she mean : whatever happens? The result of the tests, she said. She knew he needed a break, the winter had been long and he had been cooped up with her. He did not feel cooped up, he jumped in to say; he loved this little flat, and she knew it. But he might not wish to live with her for ever. She sighed. Of course *she* would not live for ever. The conversation was a repeat of earlier ones, spaced at intervals over the years, and they had always made him smile a little inside for he had known the source of her anxiety and loved her the more for it. Why should he not love his mother for loving him? This time he did not feel like smiling. Emily, he knew, suspected the pain to be a means of blackmail, a way of preventing him from taking off, but how could one ever be sure? One could be sure of nothing, said Emily, of course not; but perhaps one must be prepared to take risks at times. He did not know what he would do if his mother's pain turned out to be serious, if it was the first sign of an illness which might be terminal. She had done so much for him, as he had said to Emily, and made so few demands.

With an extra effort he cleared his plate, and she relaxed a little, sat back, allowed him to pour her a small whisky. He put on some music, built up the fire. Her hands slid back to her lap. She asked him about church that morning, who had been there, what the theme of the sermon had been, for she herself had not felt up to going. He might ask the priest to drop in and see her sometime.

At tea-time, getting up to prepare his meal which he did not want, she winced, and doubled over suddenly. He went to her. 'You are in pain, aren't you?' He saw beads of sweat standing around the greying hairline, about the pale mouth. He must call the doctor. She protested but he did and the doctor came and examined her, listened to her heart and lungs, took her blood pressure, and said that there was no cause for immediate alarm, but when she went to the Infirmary on the following day they would do their tests and see if they could determine anything further.

'Rest, Mrs McCreedy. Take it easy. No sewing for a week or two. You're not as young as you used to be, you know.'

He stood on the cold landing with Conal for a moment, outside the door of the flat. 'I think you should try to get her to slow up on her work. Does she need to work so hard?' He looked levelly at Conal. 'Isn't it about time she retired?'

'When I retire I should like to take a long trip through the States,' said Farquhar.

He and Louisa were walking in the grounds of Lauriston Castle looking out across the green sweep of the lawns down to the Forth. They had the garden to themselves; no one else appeared to be brave enough to face the March wind. Already the month was less lamb-like, thought Louisa.

He had never been to North America, or South America either, for that matter. He supposed he had really been to very few places, now that he came to think of it, had lived within a small orbit. 'I was born, bred and schooled in Edinburgh, even went to university here, no choice really on that score when one wants to do law, Scots law. Must seem amazing to you who have moved around so much?' Louisa, who had gone at various times on expeditions to Turkey and Afghanistan, said that she understood very well how it had come about. It was part of his inheritance, as moving around had been part of hers.

They turned down a different path and he offered her his arm. 'But I would like to see a bit more of the world.' He had always wanted to see the Grand Canyon and the Rockies and the Pacific Ocean. 'We might do those after the castles, eh?'

'That would be fun,' said Louisa.

Camilla buzzed around the kitchen like a fly unable to settle. Her mother sat at the table drinking coffee and gazing through the window at a point in the middle of the garden which contained nothing more interesting than a stunted, dormant rose bush.

'Are you listening to me, Mother?'

'Yes, dear, I am. Sorry.' Her mother shifted her gaze. 'I'm afraid that it sounds as if you should give Carl up, dear. I know it'll be hard for you but in the long run . . .' She was struggling, doing her best to give advice which she felt ill-equipped and, also, disinterested to give. It was Camilla's life: that was what she wanted to, but could not, say. 'When it comes to a certain point . . .'

'You and Father came to a certain point years ago but you didn't separate.'

Camilla was so illogical to converse with that it became almost distressing. No point in reminding her of the numerous occasions when she had upbraided her mother for staying with a marriage which had become sterile. No point in saying that she and Carl were not married. No point in saying that Farquhar had never wanted her to leave, whereas Carl did not want Camilla to stay. No point in saying anything.

'It might just be a bad patch,' said Camilla desperately.

'It might.'

'You don't care, do you?'

'What would you like me to say, Camilla?'

If she was going to be like that she might just as well go, said Camilla. She marched out of the kitchen to pull on her Wellingtons. She came back throwing a kind of horse blanket around her shoulders. For a change there was a flush of pink in her cheeks and a spark in the amber-coloured eyes. She held her head high.

'You might be interested to know that I'm pregnant,' she said.

Chapter Thirteen

'I DON'T want a kid. And now you can go ahead and call me a cold-hearted bastard as well if you want to!' It was the last thing that Emily wished to do, had not come for that purpose at all, but could not speak anyway, for Carl was wound up like the spring of a clock and must say everything he wished to say before he would simmer down. 'I've always told her I didn't want a kid, I've never misled her.' He paced the floor, two steps up and back, kicking the bedcovers and newly arrived bundles of clothes which were awaiting sorting. 'As far as I knew she was on the pill. As far as I knew she was taking it every night. As far as I knew!' He took a swipe at a Victorian nightdress and kicked it high up into the air. They watched its flight. On its downward journey it got caught on a hook and there remained suspended, looking dejected. Much darned too, Emily observed. But undoubtedly genuine, and as such should fetch a fair price.

Eventually, Carl ran down and sat opposite her on the other side of the paraffin heater. The fumes were bad today, catching at their throats.

'What the hell am I supposed to do now, Emily? I refuse to play daddy.'

And he would not marry her, whatever role he did finish by playing : he had no need to state that. He said what about a drink, he could use one badly? There was nothing in the cupboard so he would nip along the road if she would mind the shop. It was hardly likely anyone would come in on a Monday morning. She sat by the heater feeling slightly woozy with the heat and odour. On the way here she had felt wound up also, had composed many speeches in her head about the woman having to bear the burden in the end, say what you like about women's liberation. She did not know what to say about women's liber-

162

ation now. All that she supposed she could say in all fairness was that it was Camilla's choice, for of that she was convinced. The door opened and a girl came in looking for a nightdress. Ah, she had just the thing! How fortunate! Emily jumped up and pointed out the hanging nightdress which seemed to be exactly what the girl was looking for. With the aid of an Edwardian parasol they managed to bring the piece of clothing back to earth. The girl tried it on, stood before the mirror, turning this way and that, whilst Emily, enjoyed salemanship for the first time in her life, admired the fit and declared how pretty the girl looked in it. The girl said she would take it and Emily put it in an old Woolworth's bag – they reused other people's bags – and felt a glow of achievement.

'I made a sale,' she told Carl when he returned carrying a bottle of whisky. She eyed the bottle uncertainly. Drinking in the morning. What next? Carl said this was no ordinary morning, which she could not deny. He fetched two cups from the back room.

'We always seem to run to alcohol in times of stress,' said Emily. 'We Scots are bad that way, aren't we? One of the worst alcoholic rates in the world.' Then she remembered that Carl was English. At least, he had come from somewhere down there originally, hadn't he? Eastbourne, he said; but he was half-Dutch. 'How interesting,' said Emily, sipping her whisky, feeling its warmth seep down through her; she had always believed the Dutch to be sober and efficient. And no doubt they were, most of them, or they would not have acquired their reputation. His relatives lived in the north-east of Holland, in the province of Drenthe. 'They're half-Indonesian.' Then that explained it! She had always thought he was a little dark looking. She did not mean that as an insult, and he did not take it as one.

Then she told him about her West Indian artist.

'I always knew you hadn't lived a straight-down-the-centre life! I said so to Cammie once but she wouldn't believe me. She said you'd come from a "good" Edinburgh family and never strayed off the straight-and-narrow in your life.'

'Daughters can not be expected to know much about their mothers,' said Emily.

She did not tell him about Conal, though was tempted to, but she could not – and there was no reason why she should expect to – rely on his discretion.

'So he painted you, did he? You haven't got any of the pictures?' Carl thought that was unfortunate, but she was not so sure. To have to see herself now as she was then? It might be too painful. But she had to admit that at times she was curious, would love to see one of them once again, for she had forgotten what she did look like as a girl and when she looked at photographs she seemed to be facing a different person, studying an image that brought no echoes back whatsoever. A painting would be different, or so she fancied. 'What happened to his pictures?' Oh, he had sold them, most of them, though she hoped he might have taken at least one back with him and had it hanging now on the wall of his tropical house. That was how she always thought of him: in tropical heat, with vividly coloured plants hanging down from the verandah on which he would be sitting rocking to and fro. 'Drinking rum?' suggested Carl, and they laughed. His hair would be grizzled white now though, and that she could not imagine. She saw him eternally young. 'As he must see you?' But he might not even be alive any more, and she was here not to talk about herself but Camilla. Ah yes, Camilla. They sobered.

Carl sighed, was sorry, but what the hell could he do? Possibly nothing, agreed Emily, though he could not escape the fact that the child was his as well as Camilla's. So, O.K., then as the father of this embryo he did have some responsibility, but did Emily really want him to marry Camilla?

'I feel so sorry for my daughter, Carl. You have no idea!'

Christ, she was making him feel awful! He refilled the cups.

'I didn't come to do that. But don't you see – she had to take the pill and now *she* has to have the baby or the abortion?'

'All right, I'll marry her, Emily, if you want it.'

'I don't want it. I think it would be disastrous. You'd be in the divorce court within two years, or writing letters to it, or whatever it is they do now.'

'You agree with me then? That she should have an abortion?'

'The decision will have to be hers, Carl. I refuse to influence her in any direction. The responsibility for me would be too great, you must see that!'

The responsibility for Conal would be great if the results of his mother's tests were bad and he departed for France. She came back from the Infirmary and lay on the chaise longue, saying the experience had been degrading and humiliating. They had shoved tubes up every part of her. She would rather die than go through all that again. There came a point when dignity was more important than survival.

'I feel as if it was all my fault,' he said to Emily, when they met for a quick drink in a pub in the Grassmarket. He did not like to leave his mother alone for more than a few minutes.

Emily did not mind too much that Conal could not stay longer; she longed to crawl into the narrow bed and take a long nap before facing the evening meal. Her sisters-in-law were expected and Louisa was preparing a meal. It was the whisky consumed that morning with Carl that had made her so sleepy. She yawned, had to apologise to Conal, and explain.

'Poor Emmie. You have your own problems. You don't think this business with Camilla will stop you getting to France?'

Not at all, she declared, reviving; she intended to see that it did not. She considered her daughter old enough to cope on her own for two months. Or longer, she added to herself, for she believed that once away, they would not come back, not for a long time. People adapted to everything, given time; and they could give Mrs McCreedy time, and Farquhar, and Camilla.

She arrived home to find Camilla sleeping in her bed. She regarded the bed as hers now, saw her daughter as an interloper. Camilla stirred, opening her eyes, and looked up at her mother.

'I've come home.'

'Your father – '

'You wouldn't let him throw me out into the street?'

She allowed Camilla to go back to sleep. She had no intention of telling Farquhar anything yet, she informed Louisa, who was wearing a blue and white butcher's apron and muttering over a cookery book beside the kitchen stove.

'Farquhar's not an unreasonable man, Emily. He wouldn't put his daughter out. You don't think he would, do you?'

'No, not if it came to the crunch. But I don't believe for a moment that Camilla wishes to come back here to live. It's merely another move in her little strategy.'

And within half an hour Carl phoned to ask if Camilla was there; she had left a somewhat ambiguous note on the mantelpiece. She was here all right, said her mother, hearing the front door opening and Farquhar's throat being cleared. He had a habit of clearing his throat whenever he entered the house, as if to announce his arrival. He would now be putting his hat on the hallstand, easing off his heavy overcoat. Then he would call out her name.

'Anyone at home?' she heard him say. Ah, she had been wrong! She smiled.

'What now?' Carl was asking.

They must wait and see; Camilla could stay in the meantime but Emily would not be surprised if she got up and found Camilla gone and an ambiguous note propped up on her mantelpiece.

'I must go now.'

'I am sorry, Emily. For everything.'

Farquhar and Louisa were having a sherry, he seated at the end of the kitchen table, she standing by the draining board, her hands covered in flour and mustard.

'Seems to be quite a hive of industry in here,' said Farquhar cheerfully. 'Sherry, Emily?'

She refused. At that moment she would have been prepared to sign the pledge.

'Everything under control, Louisa?'

'Just fine.'

'Good.'

She escaped, went upstairs. She could not go to the bedroom belonging to herself and Farquhar, nor to Camilla's, or the best spare room which Louisa now occupied. That still left three. How extravagant they were, when people were living in one measly room in London for twenty pounds a week with water dripping through the roof and vermin scrabbling around their heads at night! Television programmes were full of such people. Farquhar was always saying they must move but laziness had prevented any move so far and now she no longer cared for she would not be living in this solid Victorian villa much longer. He could do what he wished, buy a bungalow at Ravelston, a country cottage in East Lothian, or a mud hut in Arabia. Or a tower house in Aberdeenshire, she thought suddenly, and smiled.

She went into a room that had not been used for many months. She lifted the eiderdown, slid beneath, and within minutes was asleep.

Camilla wakened before her mother and went downstairs to find her father and the American laughing together in the kitchen. Half-cut, she thought. 'Where's Mother?' she asked, and her father answered, 'Around somewhere,' as if he did not care. Louisa got up and stirred a mixture in a saucepan and Farquhar watched her with eyes like a spaniel's. Surely he could not be falling for that woman? Although maybe he was ready to fall for any woman when he had lived such a sexless life for so many years with her mother. She knew her mother and father had lived without sex for a long time; she had overheard a conversation one night when she had got up to go to the bathroom and had squatted on the landing in the dark listening to them. Neither her father nor Louisa were paying any attention to her. She longed for Carl to come and take her back to their little flat with its red-painted furniture and all the funny little bits and pieces they had collected together.

'I hate this stuffy ugly house,' she said loudly, but no one heard.

When the doorbell rang she ran to answer it, her heart thumping. And then it slowed again for on the doorstep stood her two aunts in belted mackintoshes and sensible shoes smiling through the rain. She pushed past them, ran round the side of the house and jumped on her bicycle.

Emily was wakened by Louisa gently shaking her shoulder. Elspeth and Davina had arrived, and Camilla had flown. From below rose succulent smells.

'You are the most fantastic cook, Louisa.'

'Do you know, Em, I really believe I am quite domesticated? I love cooking and even shining up the house gives me pleasure. I never would have believed it before.' She had never had the chance to believe it, having lived all her life in small urban apartments where scope was limited and she had been out all day struggling to make a career.

167

'Do you know, Louisa, I don't believe I am too domesticated? After a lifetime, almost, of playing at being so.' She thought that she might like to cook small meals, but only for two, and clean in a limited way, in a circle round them. Perhaps at heart she was rather a slut. There was a vogue at the moment for confessing to sluttery, was there not, or there had been? She usually found she was a little out of date, one step back in the stages of development, but that did not trouble her.

'The trouble,' said Louisa, sitting down on the bed, 'is establishing early enough what one is.'

'I agree totally. That is why I must let Camilla have some time and scope to find out.'

The door opened tentatively. 'Ah, there you both are,' said Farquhar.

'Coming,' said Louisa and went, leaving Emily to rise at leisure, change, wash her face. She felt spoiled as she combed her hair and prepared to join them downstairs for dinner.

The meal was a great success; even the aunts ate more than usual and because of that drank more wine also. Farquhar opened an extra bottle. Quite a gay evening, really, thought Emily, considering the make-up of the gathering.

Mrs McCreedy had insisted that Conal go to his performance. The show must go on! 'And you know I never mind you going out of an evening. You can't let other folk down, Conal.' She was firm on that, had brought him up to consider others; and she would be fine, promised to rest, not move, work, do anything ill-advised.

'You'll come straight back though?'

He promised.

She felt easier when he had gone; the pain lessened a little. He needed his outlets and she liked him to have as many performances in the year as possible. Before he went out he had done a little shoe shuffle in front of the hearth for her to make her laugh. It reminded her of his da. She was feeling a bit nostalgic tonight, due to the pain perhaps. She rummaged in an old shoe box under her bed and brought out some old theatre programmes and snapshots. He had been a good-looking fella, Gerry McCreedy, whatever else you could say about him, and she could say much if she was feeling vengeful. He had been a terrible man for the ladies, never seemed to be able to get enough of them. Conal had his looks but much more character, a better chin, and a stronger face altogether. Much stronger. She put the shoe box away.

She was restless now. Conal would not be home for a while and the television did not interest her. She went through to his room wanting to feel near to him. She looked around at the pictures on his walls, touched the objects that he'd gathered in the junk and antique shops. He had taste, her boy, and the women had given him some good pieces too. An oil painting given from Mrs Allen, a statue sculpted in bronze from Mrs Stewart . . .

She stopped at the table beside his bed. His passport lay on top of a pile of books. Her heart made an alarming jump and she had to breathe deeply to control it. She lifted the passport, turned it over, fingered the embossed gold crest. Was he really going to go away? Only for a holiday, he said; ten days or a fortnight. She knew she should allow him, that she would make a big mistake by trying to prevent him. Beneath was a book, the one about France he had been reading. She went back to the other room for her magnifying glass. *The Rivers of France*. She flipped through the pages. It was an old book, had been bought second-hand, bore a pencilled price inside the fly page. She paused at a picture of a place called Villeneuve. Words were written in pencil beneath it. She peered, held the glass closer. 'This is where we shall shop', it said. She turned another page, saw another note in the margin. 'Should be sunny in May. And not bad in April either'. April and May! He was not planning then to go for ten days. She knew he had lied to her, always had been able to tell when he told her less than the truth. Less than the truth : that was what he tried to make it when he had something to conceal.

When he came home he found her in bed in the recess of her room. Normally she waited up for him. Tonight they would not have their drink by the fire. She was sorry. Her voice sounded reduced, her spectacles lay on the bedside table, her exposed eyes looked red.

'You must give up sewing, Mother. I'll have to get a full-time job.'

'Nonsense, son. You can't do nine to five.'

He would get something less restricted, there must be jobs, representing firms, selling, where you could make your own hours. Him a salesman? Selling brushes door to door, or encyclopaedias? There were higher classes of salesmen, he reminded her, and she reminded him that he had no experience of anything but acting. And that was too difficult a profession for him to break into now, at his age. Anyway, she hated to think of him in bit parts, desperate for work, hanging around, toadying. She hesitated. There might be another solution. He came and sat on the edge of the bed.

'Mrs Stewart is looking for a kind of chauffeur-companion.'

But he could not drive. She thought the driving would be the least of it and, anyway, Mrs Stewart would pay for lessons for him. What she really wanted was a lackey, someone to do her bidding when she bid, he said bitterly. That was how most jobs were, said his mother. And Mrs Stewart was wealthy and most generous and would not tax him in the way that some of the other ladies he had served would.

She stretched forth her hand and clasped his tightly. 'Think about it, please, Conal. We cannot starve and perhaps the doctor is right – I may not be able to sew much longer.'

Chapter Fourteen

CAMILLA kept running to the kitchen sink to be sick and clogging the grid. Why couldn't she go to the loo? asked Carl, irritably. He was painting an old frame with gilt paint, the smell of which she claimed was nauseating her.

'I haven't time to get that far.'

'It's only another two bloody steps.'

'I hate you, do you know that? I fucking well hate you!'

Nobody was asking her to stay then; she knew he would say that. She sat down beside the sink. He didn't care did he if the paint made her feel sick, did he? He was so damned selfish he would just carry right on and do what he wanted to do. He was doing this to earn their living, he reminded her, not because it was his favourite occupation. That was screwing the redhead in the next street, wasn't it? He threw the frame across the room, splintering and rendering it irredeemable for ever. She burst into tears.

Emily arrived shortly afterwards with a bottle of sparkling wine. She had to wait for a minute or two before they opened the door and when they admitted her she realised what had caused the delay. Camilla was fastening her skirt and the bed was crumpled. Carl looked as if he did not know what was happening to him.

'I don't know what you think we've got to celebrate,' said Camilla, eyeing the bottle and Emily thought that when she got her daughter in a quieter, more receptive mood, she must tell her that she was making a habit of making sour remarks, often when she did not really want to.

'I thought we might cheer ourselves up.' It was raining very steadily, the kind of rain they seldom had, heavy, bouncing, relentless rain, which soaked you as you crossed the street. She was waiting to go and meet Conal, who at this moment would be

171

accompanying his mother to the doctor's surgery to get the result of her check-up.

Carl eased the cork off with a satisfying plop. Camilla said she'd better not have any or she'd vomit. All the more for them then, said Carl, who was building his own mechanisms of defence. It really was hopeless for them, thought Emily, even if they did still enjoy going to bed together. That would not get them through a year, let alone any resemblance of a lifetime.

'How's business, Carl?' She had taken a sudden interest since selling the nightdress and had even wondered if she and Conal might start up a small place in France selling *brocantes*. There seemed to be a market for old things in all overdeveloped societies.

'Lousy. People don't come out in bad weather. Except for other dealers and they're not much interested in our junk.'

'It's very incestuous,' said Camilla. 'They all buy from one another.'

'I suppose there must be a let-out at some point,' said Emily.

'Matter of fact, we haven't sold anything since you flogged the nightdress, Emily,' said Carl.

'Perhaps we need your lucky touch, Mother. Couldn't you come into the shop and be Carl's mascot?'

Carl refilled Emily's glass. Camilla got up to hang over the sink. She retched but nothing came. *La Nausée.*. Emily thought fondly of the time when she had been so keen on Sartre and de Beauvoir. Everything they had done or written seemed magical to her. That had been at the time of her Trinidadian lover. It was he who had introduced her to Satre and she had been ready to fall in love with every one of his enthusiams, unlike Camilla who automatically disliked everything Carl liked, except in his absence when she quoted his words to her mother, though usually without crediting them to him.

It seemed heartless to consume a bottle of wine whilst Camilla retched but perhaps it was because of that they needed it more. The rain still beat steadily against the windows making the little room seem convivial and enveloping. Emily was looking forward to giving up her villa of nine rooms plus other quarters to live in a simple building of three rooms without running water and no carpets on the stone-flagged floors.

Farquhar Mountjoy circled the station bookstall, going round and round several times, each time pausing at a slightly different point on the circumference to eye the magazines. Closing in on the counter, he fingered one or two, flipped over some pages. The ones he fingered were different from the ones that he eyed. It was astonishing what was so openly on sale these days. For a long time he had never given them more than the most fleeting of glances. Did he dare buy one? He jingled the coins in his trouser pocket, cleared his throat. He glanced over his left shoulder. He stretched forth his hand.

'Ah, Farquhar! Going somewhere?'

He jerked his head round to see Craig Paterson bearing down on his right hand. He wiped his forehead with the back of his hand.

'Oh – er, no, not exactly. Just came into the station to buy a magazine.'

He seized one and held out some coins on the palm of his hand. The woman behind the counter removed most of them.

'I'm off to London myself. Craig was eyeing the magazine pressed against Mountjoy's chest. He frowned. 'Brides? Young Camilla thinking of getting married, eh? Amazing to think she's reached that stage already.'

How time goes by . . .

They parted, Craig Paterson to catch the London train, Farquhar Mountjoy to climb the Waverley steps up to Princes Street. In the first rubbish bin he passed he dumped the magazine, cursing. You couldn't even buy a bloody magazine in this damned city without being seen.

He walked back to his office through the pouring rain. He arrived drenched, for he had forgotten to take his raincoat, to find his secretary in a state of agitation. She had stopped smiling.

'What it is, Miss Lyall?' The panic in her eyes alarmed him. He took a step forward and almost put his hands on her shoulders. He let them drop to his sides. 'Is it your mother?'

'It's twenty past twelve, Mr Mountjoy!'

Appalled, he took the silver watch from his pocket. She was right. In all the years she had worked for him he had never known her to be wrong, about anything.

He should have offered for an expensive property at Easter Belmont on behalf of an important client that morning. Offers had closed at twelve noon.

'They don't know much, these doctors,' said Mrs McCreedy as she rode home in a taxi with her son. The gutters were running with water.

'Oh, I wouldn't say that, Mother.'

'They make mistakes all the time. Mrs Allen was just telling me they diagnosed gall-stones for her sister-in-law and she died two days later of peritonitis.'

'Here,' said Conal, leaning forward to speak to the driver.

The taxi double parked alongside Mrs Stewart's Mercedes. Conal paid off the driver and helped his mother out. Mrs Stewart appeared at their side with an umbrella, and between them they helped Mrs McCreedy to the door and up the stairs. The lobby smelled of dampness and tom cat. The sun might well be shining in south-west France, thought Conal.

Conal made a pot of tea whilst his mother sat with her feet on the fender and told Mrs Stewart everything the doctor had said and not said. She was convinced he was concealing something.

'You make an excellent cup of tea, Conal,' said Mrs Stewart.

'I taught him early. There's a few things I've taught that'll stand him in good stead.'

Conal drained his cup in one swallow and refilled it.

Mrs Stewart said that she had come to pay her bill.

'That's far too much,' Mrs McCreedy protested, looking at the cheque.

'Not at all. You charge too little, Mrs McCreedy. Let us put it like that.' She turned to Conal. 'Have you thought over my offer yet, Conal?'

He hesitated, and his mother said, 'I'm sure – '

Mrs Stewart cut in, saying, 'Take your time. There's no rush. I know you must have a number of factors to consider. By the way, I have two tickets for the Baroque Ensemble next week. I know you are fond of the group . . .'

He was sorry but he could not accept since he was uncertain about his plans. She said he could change his mind any time he wished.

'She's a great woman, Mrs Stewart, so she is,' said Mrs McCreedy, after she had gone. 'She says she'll never remarry, that she'll remain faithful to the memory of her late husband. I admire that, Conal.' She was unfolding a dress of amber-coloured velvet. 'Guess who this is for!' The doorbell rang. 'Go let her in!'

Conal brought Mrs Allen back in to the room. She pulled a wet scarf from her golden-red hair and shook it free. She laughed, pleased it seemed with the wet day. She was always in good spirits when she came.

'Oh, don't go, Conal! Stay and see my dress on, tell me what you think. You know I always value your opinion.'

'He has good taste, has Conal, I will say that for him,' said his mother, holding the amber velvet, ready to lift it over the red-gold head. Mrs Allan stood before the fire in a coffee-coloured lace slip, slit low between the breasts. She had a creamy pale skin, unblemished by childbearing stretch marks or the ravages of old age. He knew without having to look at it. She pouted a little at his back. The dress slid down, was eased gently around the slender figure of the customer. Apart from the American woman, Mrs Allan's measurements were the smallest in the dressmaker's note-book. She came not due to an inability to buy off-the-peg but because she liked individually styled clothes. Also, she enjoyed coming to Mrs McCreedy. And she enjoyed Conal. Her husband was a coarse man, she had confided to the dressmaker over fittings; he had money but totally lacked sensitivity.

'Well, Conal, and what do you think?'

He must turn now. He saw her standing before the fire in the amber-coloured dress, her arms held out a little at each side, her long beautiful neck stretched slightly backward. He had often seen her neck stretched back, had put his lips against the smooth skin of her throat. She was smiling at him. She looked beautiful. He had to tell her so.

'Thank you, Conal.'

The doorbell rang again, giving him an opportunity to leave

the room. On the landing stood Louisa, soaking wet, holding a parcel. She was hoping his mother might make something up for her. He took her into the living room.

His mother was in the middle of helping Mrs Allan off with the dress.

'Sorry,' cried Louisa. 'I don't want to intrude.'

Over the half-raised dress Mrs Allan smiled at her. 'Don't worry about me. Carry on, Mrs McCreedy.'

The dressmaker removed the dress. Her mouth was puckered tight as if it held a cushionful of pins. Mrs Allan remained standing in her slip, making no move to replace her clothes. Conal introduced her and Louisa and Louisa noticed the way in which Mrs Allan looked at Conal.

'I won't shake hands. I'm just dripping wet. Gosh, I'm leaving a puddle all over your carpet, Mrs McCreedy.'

'I don't recall you having an appointment, Miss Grant.'

Louisa said that she didn't, but had been hoping, well, to take advantage of Mrs McCreedy's good nature. She began to unwrap the sopping brown paper but Mrs McCreedy said very firmly that she was taking no more orders just now, on doctor's orders. And she still had one garment to finish for Miss Grant anyway.

'Oh, I'm sorry. Did you get bad news?'

Louisa received no answer for Mrs McCreedy was edging her out, saying that she must attend to her client and was sure Miss Grant would understand. She would not allow Conal to get between them. The two in the room heard the front door slamming and then the dressmaker came back.

'What an ill-mannered young woman! Coming barging in like that, no thought for anybody...'

Mrs Allan's eyes had not left Conal's face.

'Have you acquired any new pieces of Art Nouveau recently, Conal?'

'There's that nice little brass tray you brought home the other day.'

Conal was sure that Mrs Allan would not be interested in that.

'I'd just adore to see it.' Mrs Allan was already walking towards the door. She had a languorous walk, one which Mrs McCreedy much admired. It was the way women should walk instead of barging about like that stupid American woman. From the door she looked back. 'Aren't you coming to show it to me, Conal?'

Conal went.

Mrs McCreedy sat down at her sewing machine, fitted a piece of cloth under the foot, and put her foot on the treadle. Then she let her foot fly. And as she sewed she hummed and smiled.

She was surprised when the door opened but a moment later. Mrs Allan entered, less languorously, and began to put on her clothes.

'Didn't you like the tray, Mrs Allan?'

'Conal was right – it wasn't of any interest to me.' Her voice was clipped, and no longer soft. She left quickly.

Mrs McCreedy moved to the fire and after a while Conal came back asking if she would like more tea, or was there anything else he could get for her?

'I hope you didn't offend Mrs Allan in any way, son. She's one of my best customers, you know. I wouldn't like to lose her.'

'You're to cut down on your customers, the doctor said so.'

'But I'd like to choose the ones I keep. I want to keep Mrs Allan and I don't want that American.' When she had finished the dress she was making for her she did not intend to set eyes on her again.

'All right, Mother, all right! You don't have to set eyes on anyone you don't want to. But you must not get worked up.'

He sat down. He had been thinking. She clasped her hands together, not liking the sound of that. Was it not time she retired completely? This flat was so many floors up too : that was another thing. The older she got the steeper the climb would seem, and the more difficult to go out. She had always talked of going back to Ireland one day, hadn't she? Everyone talked of going back to Ireland, she said sharply. But he had written to her sister Maeve in Monaghan. He pulled an envelope from his pocket and took out a single sheet of ruled lilac paper. 'Tell Mary she is always welcome here. I am often lonely and she would be good company. As you know, I have the spare room. It was freshly papered only last year by your cousin Dermot. I look forward to hearing again. God look to you both. Loving thoughts always, Aunt Maeve.'

The flames crackled; Conal replaced the sheet in its lilac envelope; Mrs McCreedy tightened the clasp of her hands till the knuckles showed white.

'She's got a right nice wee cottage, Mother, and you'd know everyone in the village. A number of your relatives are still living there. We could sell this flat and you'd have the income from that to live on, plus your pension.'

She moistened her lips with the edge of her tongue. 'And where would you be, son?'

'I thought I might travel for a while.'

'Travel?'

'Before it's too late. Well, I'm not as young as I used to be either, am I now?' He laughed.

She understood, she said, and did not wish to tie him. But she did not want to go back to Monaghan where she knew everyone.

'You couldn't stay here alone, Mother.'

'So you are determined to go?'

'I want to go.'

Consider it, he pleaded; once she got used to the idea it would not seem so bad and he would come to visit her regularly. Like Christmas and Easter, she supposed. Oh, more than that, he assured her, but she was not to be reassured. She would be lucky if she saw him twice a year when the Irish Sea divided them; and then after a while it would be once, and then not even that, She had seen it happen all too often.

She would lie down now; the day had drained her.

'You *must* let me lead my own life, Mother. I have stayed with you for a long time, longer than most – '

Oh, she knew, she knew! He did not have to tell her. And now was she to get down on her knees in gratitude and thank him for his sacrifice?

'It hasn't been a sacrifice. We've had good times but now – '

Now her good times were to be over, she was to be shoved into a cottage with her sister Maeve who'd been boring enough with her addiction to the Virgin Mary at the age of seven so God alone knew what she would be like at seventy! She'd have them on their knees from morning to night and would pray so long over the dinner table that your dinner would be frozen stiff before you

178

ever got at it. And those blue and gold pictures of hers everywhere would give you the dry bokes. Conal had said that himself often enough. He used to say she must have won them at a coconut shy run by sky-blue nuns. He could never wait to get away when they went there for their holidays. He used to say the place smelt of priests and cats.

'I know what I used to say!' He lowered his voice, but spoke no less firmly. 'But I am saying something different now, Mother.'

Emily stayed at Carl and Camilla's until it was time to go and meet Conal. She did some washing and ironing which had been lying around for a few weeks, saying she was quite happy to be of some practical help and felt too restless to sit down.

'What are you restless about?' asked Camilla.

Emily looked out at the rain and smiled.

Camilla walked down to the car with her, stood in the rain. She was getting wet deliberately, thought her mother, subconsciously trying to increase the pathos of her state.

'Go, in, Camilla! You'll catch a chill.'

'I'm sure Carl's getting ready to leave me, Mother.'

'I doubt if he would skip off, just like that. He's quite a civilised young man.'

'You didn't use to think so.'

'One can always change one's mind, Camilla.' She kissed her daughter's wet cheek, took her shoulders and squeezed them. 'If you need any money to help you out . . .'

'Money! You think that solves everything, don't you?'

'No, I don't. Far from it. But it could help you. You might need it.'

Driving away, she saw the blurred reflection of her daughter in the mirror. She was standing quite still watching her drive away.

'You're wet,' said Conal, putting his hands around her head as he ducked into the car beside her.

'Who isn't today?' She looked searchingly at him. 'Your mother's all right?'

He nodded. Every X-ray had been clear, every check had registered as normal. The specialists had found nothing, except signs of old age of course. And they were not anything to get alarmed over. They had said she was surprisingly fit, except for her eyes.

'So we shall go to France after all?'

'We will, Emmie! My mind is made up. I've told my mother – oh, not exactly that – but other things.'

'Good. I knew you would.'

Davina and Elspeth, passing in mackintoshes and galoshes, recognising Emily's car, knocked on the window, but their knocking was not heard.

Chapter Fifteen

'I THINK it's time we had a talk, Emily,' said Farquhar. It was with relief that she heard him say the words, ones which she had felt must inevitably come; and yet day after day he had said nothing, had looked reproachfully at her at times, at others not, but regarded her more with an air of disinterestedness.

They went into the study. She sat; he stood with his hands behind his back.

'Rumours have been reaching me . . .' What he had to say was not easy and she knew that she must help him. She nodded, denying nothing, finishing off a sentence or two here and there, but she could not volunteer any direct information either. *I am having an affair with a man young enough to be my son.* That he might not wish to hear articulated. She had been seen around the town in various places – in Edinburgh it was impossible to be clandestine – but no one, she was sure, had ever seen her in, what Farquhar would call, a compromising position. She smiled, remembering how she had lain between the orchids in the hothouse. He saw her smile and frowned. Quickly she became serious again.

'This young fellow – '

'Conal.'

'Mm. He's an actor, isn't he?'

'I have become very fond of him, Farquhar.'

He cleared his throat, shuffled his feet up and down the Turkish rug. It was a very old one, of beautiful shades of red and clay and turquoise and green. She would take it with her, lay it on the stone-flagged floor. She would be entitled to take something after all.

'And he's fond of you too, I take it? Although I must say – ' He did not say but she knew what bewildered him: a young man appeared to be in love with his wife. More shuffling and

181

throat-clearing, and some sighing, and then he said, more firmly, 'It seems to me that things haven't been too good between us for quite a long time, Emily. Years, in fact.' She nodded, felt a tension ease within her chest. Just to hear him admit it! Rather than to have to go on with the terrible play they had been acting out for almost a decade. The devoted Mountjoys solidly together when everyone else was crumbling and falling apart. He went on to say things about it not seeming to be unusual these days, quite different from their parents' day of course, almost like an infectious disease, all very messy and what an upheaval it caused in families. At least their children were off their hands. That was something. They wouldn't suffer.

'You think we ought to separate then, Farquhar?'

'Hardly seems worth staying together if we feel like this, does it? I'm still fond of you, Emily, but –'

Again she nodded: she understood. For the first time in their lives they felt exactly the same. Perhaps that was not literally true, she thought, but almost. At the point of parting. For a moment she felt a pang, a deep thrust of anguish turning in the centre of her, regret that they had had to end this way. And later when she went to bed alone she would weep into her pillow. But now she must be unwavering and businesslike for Farquhar wished to discuss practical matters, make arrangements, come to an agreement on the division of their material goods.

'If I could just have one or two things –'

'Don't be ridiculous! You are entitled to half the house. Of course! You've looked after it and me and the children all these years. I wouldn't have it otherwise.'

She had expected nothing. His generosity – for it was as such she saw it though knew that rationally what he said made sense – brought her first stirrings of guilt. Amazingly, up until now, she had felt none. Where had her Presbyterian soul fled to? she had asked Louisa. She wanted to confess now, to say, 'I am guilty. I am the guilty party.' But one look at Farquhar's face showed he feared being cast in the role of priest-confessor and she had no right to inflict that on him. Nor was he wishing to lay claim to innocence himself. She said, 'Thank you for the offer, Farquhar. I appreciate it.'

It was about time they sold the place anyway, he had always meant to do something long before this, and now it must be worth fifty thousand. So she would have twenty-five, plus half the furniture, and her car. 'As regards maintenance –'

'Please no, Farquhar, I don't wish you to support me any longer.'

But what would she live on? She had never had a job in her life and that was as much his fault as hers as he had not wanted her to work when they married, would have been affronted to feel that he could not support his own wife. He still believed that a man wasn't fit to marry until he could support a woman. Which brought him to the sticky subject of Conal and his inability to support her, for obviously he could not.

'We might start a small business together on my twenty-five thousand.'

Business? What did she know of that world? And what kind of business was she referring to? She liked his tone less now but could not blame him for it. She said that she might like to buy and sell antiques or second-hand books and he said that Edinburgh was coming down with such places, it was a wonder half of them made a living. Look at Carl and Camilla and their torn flannel petticoats! It need not be on that level, she replied, and it need not be in Edinburgh either. She and Conal thought of going to France where they could buy a house still at a cheap price, invest the remaining money, live simply, and perhaps do some trade in the antique market.

'There are all sorts of possibilities, Farquhar!' she cried. 'I don't know yet what I shall do. And Conal is a good actor as well as being strong and –'

'Young,' finished Farquhar.

'Yes, he is comparatively young. But no adolescent.'

He thought she was unrealistic, envisaged her starting up all manner of crazy activities like growing mushrooms, shipping back Louis XIV furniture, and going hopelessly broke. She didn't even seem to care. He sounded grudging, almost as if he envied her, for he would always need to be secure.

'I feel confident I should never starve.'

'I would never let you, Emily.'

She recognised that and was grateful.

183

'But you, Farquhar – Will you be all right?'

He considered so. She must not worry about him. He would buy a small flat, probably in the New Town, Moray Place, or somewhere like that. Three rooms would do him. Would he not be lonely? She wanted to probe but must move gently. He shrugged. They hadn't done much together anyway, had they, these last few years? No, she supposed not. But they had brought up the children, shared those anxieties, and pleasures, and they must not forget that. *'Don't* forget that, dear.' He looked embarrassed to hear her call him dear now, as if the separation, and divorce, had already taken place. He said that after two years they could divorce on grounds of breakdown of marriage with the minimum of fuss. She realised that he had given more thought to the future than she : she had not seen beyond April and May, content to have those two months, let life take its course, and wait for some sign to point the way. But Farquhar could never be passive; he must take decisions.

'Louisa out?' he asked suddenly.

'She's gone to collect a dress from Mrs McCreedy, but she should be back shortly.'

'Oh, I see. Just wondered.'

'You get on well with her, don't you?' she said, moving in.

'Tell you the truth – I've, er, become quite fond of her, Emily. Oh, nothing improprietous has taken place under our roof, you understand, you need not imagine that, not for a second –'

She did not, she said, and added, 'I am sure Louisa is fond of you also.'

'You think so?'

'I do.'

'I must seem like an old man to her.'

'There's no bigger an age gap between you and her than there is between Conal and me.'

'True, true.' He tugged at his moustache. 'And it's less important when the man's older than the woman anyway.'

'Is it?'

'Of course. Ask anyone. It's more natural.'

She got up, restless now, and went to the window, to look at the garden. The daffodils were out by the back wall.

184

'Would you like to marry her, Farquhar?'

'I am not sure she would want to marry me.'

'I don't know – she likes men of the law.'

'Yes, she does, doesn't she?' He was both pleased and troubled, not caring for the idea that he could be her fifth husband. In Scotland few had got that far yet. But of course she was American and it was different there and one must make allowances. I want to go to France, Emily was thinking, her nose against the dusty glass; I want to get away. She knew what *she* wanted to do; they must decide for themselves.

'Not that of course we have discussed anything approaching –'

She turned. 'But you might, when I'm gone. I would be pleased for you, Farquhar, if you found someone to be happy with.'

The front doorbell rang. It could hardly be Louisa, said Emily, going to answer it, unless she had forgotten her key, but it might be Camilla who had not made her visit that day yet. As soon as she saw the policeman standing on the doorstep she thought she would faint.

'What is it, Emily?' Farquhar had followed.

'Bad news.' It was written unmistakably on the young constable's face. 'Has something happened to our daughter Camilla?' she cried. Farquhar put his hands on her shoulders.

'No, madam, it's not her.'

'Conal McCreedy?' she whispered.

'Let him speak, Emily. Come inside, constable. No need to stand there freezing on the doorstep. It's a nasty day.'

The policeman took off his hat and stepped into the hall.

'Does a Miss Louisa Grant reside here?'

'She does,' said Mr Mountjoy.

'I'm afraid there's been a terrible accident, sir . . .'

There was still a small crowd gathered at the north end of the Grassmarket even though there was nothing much to see, except for a few bloodstains on the pavement. The body had been taken away before Emily and Farquhar Mountjoy arrived. A woman was staring up at the top of the tenement.

'She fell from the top window. I saw her. Honest to God, I thought my own heart would stop. She dropped like a stone. She was screaming. There was nothing you could do, nothing anybody could do.' An ambulance had come and the men had put her body, clad in a brassière and pants, on to a stretcher and covered the stretcher with a sheet. 'Poor soul. And her only in her underwear too.'

Emily buried her face in Farquhar's tweed overcoat.

'She died at once, Emily. At least that's a comfort.' The policeman had said her neck was broken.'

They skirted the crowd, entered the stair door. He kept his hand under her elbow as they mounted the steps together, steadying her when she faltered, putting his other hand against the small of her back. He stood aside from her only when she pulled the McCreedys' bell.

Conal opened the door. His face was ashen, his eyes bloodshot. 'Emily!' he cried, then drew back, on seeing Farquhar.

'Do you think we could come in for a moment, Conal?'

Before he could speak his mother called from within. 'Who is it, Conal? Who is there? Who is there?' Her voice was thin and reedy and had the rise and fall of a voice keening at a wake. Conal excused himself and whilst he was gone they listened to the voice going on and on rising and rising until it became so shrill that Emily had to put her fingers to her ears. Even Farquhar looked disquieted. He leant against the wall and half-closed his eyes.

Conal returned, came out on to the landing, closing the door to behind him. He did not have to tell them that his mother was not

'She died at once, Emily. At least that's a comfort. The police-Of course! Farquhar could well imagine, and they did not wish to add to her distress. But perhaps Conal could tell them what had happened exactly? They were still not quite clear. How could they ever be clear? wondered Emily.

It seemed that Louisa had gone to lean out of the window, as she often did when she visited the flat. Emily nodded, confirming that. Well, she must have leaned too far out: that was all. Mrs McCreedy's spectacles had come adrift – the legs were needing mended – and she had only seen a blur at the window. Then she had heard a scream, a long scream, of someone falling. Of Louisa falling. 'She was very light,' said Conal helplessly. 'I suppose she could lose balance easily. And my mother could do nothing.'

'She must be very upset,' said Farquhar. 'What a dreadful experience for her!' His own voice trembled a little though he was keeping himself well under control. 'We won't trouble you any more, Mr McCreedy.'

'Wait for me downstairs, Farquhar, will you?' said Emily. They waited until the sound of his footsteps had ceased to echo in the stair well. They looked at one another.

'Meet me tomorrow afternoon, Conal. In the Botanics, at three? Usual place.'

He nodded.

She went home with Farquhar and they drank some brandy together. 'If you'd like to talk, Farquhar – ?' He shook his head. They both went to bed early, each to their own, and both lay awake thinking of Louisa and their future lives.

Conal was at the palm house before her. He stood just inside the door. He looked as if he needed the warmth, as she did. Since the policeman had come yesterday she had felt cold, stone cold.

He took her hands, pulled her close to him.

'It's so awful – '

There was no more than that to be said. Tonight, Farquhar was going to telephone Louisa's father in the States and tell him what had happened to his daughter. He was already making tentative arrangements for a funeral, although it might be that Mr Grant would wish to take the body home. A feeling of unreality surrounded the one stark fact: that Louisa was dead. Emily and Conal clung to one another. She could not speak freely to him, say what was running in her mind, and had been all night. How could she make such a terrible accusation against his mother?

'I'm afraid now, Emily – '

She knew: he would not be able to leave his mother to go to France.

'I just couldn't. It would be the end of her.'

She could not expect him to kill his mother for her sake, indeed would find the sacrifice too much. Let them go for a walk through the gardens now. The trees were budding, a few early pink and red rhododendron blossoms beginning to appear, to look like miracles of colour after the greyness of the winter. More were waiting, ready to burst open. They walked down below the sculpture garden, looked at the city skyline ranging from the castle to the Salisbury crags, pierced by spires and cranes and towers.

'It's beautiful, isn't it?'

'Perhaps after a while, Emily –'

She did not think so. She had always known it was to be now or never. It would have to be a clean break.

'We've had our days of wine and roses, Conal,' she said.

Louisa's father did not come for the funeral. When they rang the last number under Ronald J. Grant in her address book – there were pagefuls of scored-out addresses – they got through to a rooming house in Denver, Colorado. 'Who?' the woman demanded. Farquhar repeated the name patiently. 'Oh, him! He left months ago. You don't happen to know where he is, do you?' Farquhar said that was what he wished to find out himself. 'Huh!' The edge in the woman's voice suggested he he might have left owing money, or something of that nature, so Farquhar, not wishing to get embroiled in any kind of acrimonious debate on the shortcomings of Louisa's father or to run his phone bill up on a transatlantic call to a disgruntled landlady, hastily terminated the conversation. They were left with no option but to attend to the funeral of Louisa themselves.

They asked their own minister to say a few words in the crematorium chapel. Emily and Farquhar Mountjay, the only mourners, stood side by side with bowed heads in the front row, the coffin before them. Conal had sent a note saying he had intended to come but when he had mentioned it to his mother she had become hysterical. Camilla had offered to lend moral support, as had Davina and Elspeth, which was kind of them, Emily considered, but really there was no point. Louisa had been a stranger to them, more or less. She had been a stranger to Farquhar and herself until a few weeks ago. Poor Louisa! Dying unnecessarily, a sacrificial victim paying for a crime she had not committed. A case of mistaken identity. And soon now she would be cremated, in a foreign land, and her ashes scattered on alien soil. And it was then, when it was too late, that Emily remembered that Louisa as a Catholic might have wished to be buried, intact, in consecrated ground.

'Out of a misty dream,' she murmured.

'What's that you're saying, Emily?'

'Nothing, Farquhar.'

He took her arm and led her out. Another group of mourners was waiting to use the chapel. They went home and drank more brandy together.

'Farquhar, I know how you must be feeling – '

'Emily, don't let us overstate the case, exaggerate my attachment.' She looked startled. He said, 'I was very fond of Louisa but – ' But he had not been in love with her? It had not gone that far, he answered, turning his face away, reaching out for the brandy bottle. She understood : he was not going to hold Louisa as a tragic memory in his mind; in time she would be remembered as an unfortunate incident.

'Farquhar, you remember our conversation on the day Louisa died?'

Naturally. But she had said she was not going away now with Conal, so perhaps they should forget it.

'No, we can't. I am sorry, but I can't go on living in this house any longer, don't you understand?'

Carl came the following day. Farquhar was at work, the daily help no longer came, so Emily was alone, had been since breakfast-time.

'I've just come to say goodbye, Emily. I'm going away. I know it seems bloody-minded of me but I've got to. Camilla will cling to me unless I do and she'll strangle me and herself in the end too.'

He was leaving her the shop and its stock which could hardly be accounted as much, since the shop was rented and the stock of doubtful value, depending so much on chance and whim. But it was everything he had, apart from his fare to London.

They talked a while and he thanked her for being so considerate and understanding and he almost seemed to speak in words that Farquhar might have used; the intimacy gained over the old clothes with a bottle of whisky on a wet morning could not be recaptured here. She promised to look after Camilla, see that she was all right. 'A rather futile promise, Carl, but I shall make it. I don't know what I can guarantee to do but she *is* my daughter.'

She took him to Waverley Station. A bit bizarre, she could imagine Farquhar saying, aiding and abetting the running away of their daughter's lover, but she intended to go to town anyway and she might as well give him a lift. She reached out his suitcase and wished him luck.

'You too, Emily!'

She turned up the ramp, crossed Princes Street and drove down to Stockbridge. Camilla was sitting in the middle of a heap of clothes crying.

'And if you've come to advise me to have an abortion you can bloody well go away!'

'I haven't, dear.' She cleared a chair and sat down. 'If you want to have the baby you should go ahead and have it.'

Camilla looked up. 'Even though that bugger's gone and left me?'

'Even though.'

'I do want it.'

If Louisa was here she would say Camilla's motives were questionable. Oh Christ, Louisa! Emily put her hands over her face.

'Are you all right, Mother?' Camilla came to her, knelt down.

'I'm fine, dear.' She smiled. 'And now we must make some plans.'

'You'll help me? Father couldn't cope with having me back, could he, not with a baby?'

Camilla was right: he could not. She was not proposing that; she was suggesting that she buy a flat and Camilla and she could live together with the baby. They could run the shop together too; she was willing to have a go.

Camilla sat back on her heels. 'You really mean it?'

'I'll tell you something, Camilla. When I was your age I got pregnant. Oh, it was all most unsuitable, much more so then than now, and it would have caused a great scandal. So I had an abortion, an illegal one since there was no choice. I wouldn't say I've regretted it – there's no much point in that – but I've often wondered whether I did the right thing because if I had kept the baby it would have been my chance to break what seemed to be my preordained pattern. And then for the first five years of my marriage I didn't manage to conceive and I suffered agonies thinking I might be sterile. I felt guilty too because I hadn't told your father. He wouldn't have married me if I had. So if you really do want to go ahead –'

Camilla swamped her with a hug, the first spontaneous one for many years. Perhaps she need not grow like Farquhar after all, and if she could keep this child and love him then sometime later she might meet another man whom she could love again as she had done Carl.

'But what about Father? He can't even cook or do his own laundry. You've always been a skivvy to him.'

Emily sighed. She was sorry about Farquhar but considered there was nothing she could do for him any longer, except iron his shirts and cook his porridge, which did not seem sufficient reason to stay. She saw him as solidified, set in a mould beyond her breaking. Perhaps if he had had a chance with Louisa, even for a while, he might have become more fluid, and the mould might have begun to crack. But her role as wife was exhausted now, although that of mother was going to continue for a while longer. Perhaps indefinitely. Perhaps it was a role one never could relinquish totally.

'One thing, Camilla, we must make sure we don't smother the child. It could be dangerous for him – to have two women and no man in his life. One woman with a child is difficult enough. But as long as we are aware...'

Farquhar Mountjoy sat at his desk writing words for an advertisement such as he had written many times before. Only the details varied.

'Highly-desirable, detached, stone-built villa in first-class residential area, with large walled garden to front and rear, double garage. Three reception, six beds, usual offices. Full gas-fired central heating. Suitable for family home or could be broken –'

He stopped, got up abruptly, crumpling the rug beneath the chair. He walked to the window, looked into the desirable walled garden where the lilac and gean trees were in full blossom. A ginger cat ran along the side wall and took a leap into the gean tree. He banged his fist against the window and the cat, thinking the blow was for him, leapt back on to the wall and disappeared over the other side.

Farquhar Mountjoy returned to his desk and finished writing.